In our lives, we're given countless opportunities to learn, grow and improve, with God's help and the help of family, friends, leaders and colleagues. Along the way, we often find that fulfillment is not a destination but something we experience in the never-ending process of becoming better, truer, more complete versions of ourselves. In this thoughtful and heartfelt book, local Chick-fil-A owner-operator David Grimm shares many of the timeless lessons he has learned in his life and career so far with candor, compassion and care.

Dan T. Cathy
Chairman, Chick-fil-A Inc.

"The Never-Ending Pursuit" is one of the most practical books I've ever read on living a life of purpose and genuine satisfaction. And what makes it so different is that it is filled with spiritual insights and, at the same time, teaches very sound theology. I've never read anything like this in my life. It is a must-read. It is FANTASTIC, POWERFUL, and RIVETING.

David Grimm is one of the most genuine and pure-hearted followers of Jesus I've ever met. Every pastor dreams of having people like David and Kelly Grimm and their children as parishioners. Their life story is filled with incredible and unique events. You will be deeply moved, challenged, and inspired by their life journey and the wonderful miracles shared in this incredible book.

David is a gifted author and has unique insight into spiritual truths. Much like Max Lucado, David's writings are practical and simple yet profound. This book is uniquely encouraging and yet extremely challenging all at the same time.

Reading "The Never-Ending Pursuit" will be life-changing. A GREAT BOOK!!

P.S. The study guide is excellent and very substantive. It is a terrific small group guide.

James Weaver
Founding Pastor of New Hope Assembly,
Urbandale, Iowa

As one of David Grimm's pastors, I have been able to watch and observe his life, work, and ministry from a front row seat. And I can tell you that he is the real deal! What he writes in the pages of this book are not just platitudes or cliches, David and his family live out what he talks about in "The Never-Ending Pursuit." If you want to live a successful and fulfilling life that impacts the world around you in a significant way, this book will give you the practical building blocks to make it happen. I highly recommend it to you!"

Jeff Hill
Senior Pastor
New Hope Assembly of God
Urbandale, Iowa

Dave has a compelling story, but to be brutally honest, when he told me the title, it sounded somewhat uninspiring. What's more, the thought of a journey with no end seemed mentally exhausting. Then I started reading, and before finishing the introduction I was up for the pursuit. Turning our perspective from a destination-driven mindset to the joy of the journey can put us on a path toward true satisfaction and success. With an emphasis on practicality and action, "The Never-Ending Pursuit" will inspire and equip many to press on into the adventure we call life.

Carey Huffman
Discipleship Pastor
New Hope Assembly of God
Urbandale, Iowa

In writing "The Never-Ending Pursuit," David has found a way to put to words one of the most important lessons in life... DON'T STOP!

When people get a sense of arrival, they quit growing, quit learning, quit moving, and quit mastering. But David's book, "The Never-Ending Pursuit," encourages us to GO HIGHER! Never stop. This is especially important for men or women of Faith. The moment you act like you've arrived, you'll start surrendering areas of your life to the enemy. The Never-Ending Pursuit encourages me to never stop pursuing holiness, righteousness, and faithfulness - and the story of David's life shows me that as I keep on going, I'll keep seeing God's blessing and favor in my life! But the moment I start acting like I've arrived, the blinders will go up, and the enemy will get a foothold.

This book is BRILLIANT. It is a must-read for all, but especially good for those tempted to slip into the complacency of what I call "Arrival Syndrome."

Jesse Newman
Lead Pastor
Eternity Church
Clive, Iowa

THE
NEVER-ENDING
PURSUIT

Finding Fulfillment
in Life's Journey

DAVID GRIMM

The Pursuit Press
Empowering Your Journey, One Story at a Time

ACKNOWLEDGMENTS

To my beautiful wife, Kelly, who always supports me in pursuing the dreams God has placed inside me, no matter how crazy they may seem.

To my four incredible children, Tenley, Asher, Hallie, and Sadie: never stop pursuing God for the big things He has for you!

To my Dad and Mom, Dennis and Barbara: thank you for loving me unconditionally when I was at my worst, teaching me God's Word, and always believing God had a plan for my life. Mom, I hope you can witness all God is doing here from Heaven.

To Pastor Shawn Lyons, my teacher, friend, and father in the faith: I have learned to follow Christ as you have followed Christ.

To Pastor James Weaver and Pastor Jeff Hill, thank you for welcoming me to the New Hope family with open arms and supporting our family every step of the way.

To the Chick-fil-A family, thank you for allowing me the opportunity to go through a leadership masterclass in this thing called a franchise.

To Brady Ross, thank you for helping me learn how to write books and for all your contributions!

Above all else, I thank my Lord and Savior, Jesus Christ, who gives me daily wisdom to keep pursuing what matters.

TABLE OF CONTENTS

INTRODUCTION:
THE SECRET TO TRUE HAPPINESS

I've learned why so few people are truly happy or fulfilled in life, and the reason may shock you.

It's not because they lack money, power, or success. There are plenty of rich, famous, and impactful people in the world who wouldn't claim to be "happy." At the same time, I've met people in small third-world villages with zero prestige or influence outside of their small communities who appear to be some of the most joyful people on Earth.

What separates many people from being happy is an inaccurate understanding of where true happiness comes from. Ultimately, happiness is not circumstantial. It's not something that some people are lucky enough to stumble into, while others aren't quite as fortunate.

You are in charge of your happiness. It's something you can control. At the same time, if you don't have the right mindset or understanding of how to cultivate and maintain happiness, you'll never grow beyond your current position.

The United States Declaration of Independence begins with an affirmation that each person is created with certain unalienable rights, meaning rights that cannot be taken away. Among these rights are life, liberty, and the pursuit of happiness.

To be honest, I used to interpret this claim as a disclaimer of sorts. I assumed that our Founding Fathers understood that happiness wasn't guaranteed but wanted to make clear that each person had the right to pursue happiness. If it works out, great. If not, good for you to try.

At this point in my life, I read this sentence much differently. Actually, I think guaranteeing the pursuit of happiness is better than promising happiness itself.

There is no happiness without the pursuit. I don't mean this in a chicken-and-egg sort of manner. In fact, I think that people misunderstand happiness – and struggle to find true happiness – because they don't conceptualize this critical truth.

Too many people focus on happiness as a destination. They work hard to reach a goal and enjoy the instantaneous satisfaction they experience when they accomplish what they worked to achieve. However, they are surprised when that sense of fulfillment doesn't last, and they shift their attention to work on something different.

This sense of cognitive dissonance is why Tom Brady suggested in November 2022 that he wasn't satisfied with seven Super Bowl championships, more than any individual franchise in the NFL. It's why we read about a woman in John 4 who had been married to five different men (and who kept returning to the same well to draw water). Although she could never find true fulfillment, she continued searching.

I imagine you can relate to some degree. Have you ever worked tirelessly to earn a promotion, graduate with your degree, earn an academic or athletic scholarship, start your own business, or finish a marathon? Each example represents a huge accomplishment, and I'm sure you felt an instantaneous sense of joy and satisfaction when you finished, but how long did that feeling last?

What you didn't realize was that the journey – not the destination – is where true satisfaction could be found. If life were a game, the goal wouldn't be to win. The goal would be to keep playing.

This book exists to help you appreciate the journey before – and beyond – the finish line. Yes, we all will cross that finish line one day, but how you run the race now will make all the difference when you get there. In reading, I hope and pray that you begin to take on a different perspective on life. My desire is to help you see that life isn't just about the end game - it's also about what happens in the pursuit.

As I come to grips with this reality, I see a new realm of possibility and opportunity. For starters, if life is more about the journey than the end destination, we don't have to postpone happiness. You don't have to wait to find satisfaction, fulfillment, or contentment in a single accomplishment or achievement. You can be confident in your daily efforts to bring value into the world and make your community better than it was before.

At my place of business, I always challenge my team to leave people better than they found them. Since 2015, I've owned and operated a Chick-fil-A franchise in West Des Moines, Iowa. In the past eight years as a Chick-fil-A franchise owner, I've come to deeply appreciate the value of the pursuit. One of the things I love most about Chick-fil-A is that the company doesn't just exist to serve delicious food. Our founder, Truett Cathy, once said during his life, "We should be about more than just selling chicken. We should be a part of our customers' lives and the communities we serve." This quote is still displayed proudly on Chick-fil-A's corporate website.

As a Chick-fil-A owner, I care deeply about infusing this value into the work of our local franchise. It's what motivates me to provide free college tuition for team members. It's why, as of the writing of this book, our restaurant has donated over $750,000 to our community in food donations and support, along with $150,000 in food donations to our local homeless shelters. It's why I started an online blog called "The Pursuit" in 2020, and it's why I felt driven to create the book that you're holding in your hands or viewing on your screen. I look around and see people pursuing all kinds of endeavors, but my goal is to help people learn about the only pursuit that truly matters.

As I seek to infuse these values into my work at Chick-fil-A, I recognize something incredible happening. This heightened perspective on the pursuit reminds me that growth and transformation are gradual processes. You and I will never finish the journey to become our best selves. While this may sound discouraging, it's actually a good thing. The goal isn't to arrive at one place. Instead, our objective should be continued growth and transformation each day.

In the New Testament, Jesus' followers are called "disciples." The word "disciple" comes from the Greek word "μαθητής" (mathetes), which means "learner." In the Greco-Roman world, disciples sought to implement the lifestyle and practices of their teachers fully. Quite literally, they would model each aspect of their lives after what their teachers embodied.

How appropriate is it that the calling Jesus gives us, as His followers, is not to reach a certain destination but to join Him on a journey? It's a journey full of ups, downs, twists, and turns, with no clear end destination on this side of Heaven but with a constant call to deeper faith, commitment, and self-improvement. As we read in Hebrews 12:1 (NLT), "Therefore, since we are surrounded by such a huge crowd of witnesses to the life of faith, let us strip off every weight that slows us down, especially the sin that so easily trips us up. And let us run with endurance the race God has set before us."

As disciples, we should constantly seek to align our thoughts, attitudes, and actions with what Jesus teaches. We won't always be perfect, but you'll be amazed at the transformation possible through the presence of the Holy Spirit in your lives.

You'll also develop an entirely new perspective on difficult seasons in life. You'll begin to recognize the value in struggles because you see how they help you grow and develop to become the person God has called you to be.

I'll be honest with you - I don't enjoy hard times. I don't know if anybody truly looks forward to pain and suffering. However, as I've gone through life and experienced various forms of heartbreak and trial, my attitude about these experiences has changed completely.

Several years ago, it seemed like everything around me was falling apart. I was eight years into my occupation as a youth pastor when my father contracted a strange illness. When he first began having trouble breathing, the doctors diagnosed him with pneumonia. However, things continued to get worse, and he was eventually taken by ambulance to Pittsburgh. When he arrived, he was diagnosed with Acute Myeloid Leukemia, a rare form of cancer that usually leads to death within one month of its onset.

Thanks to God's healing power expressed in cutting-edge treatments and some of the wisest doctors around, my father is still alive. However, it was a long road back, and we didn't know that the eventual outcome would be so positive. We expected the worst.

To make matters more difficult, my mother contracted breast cancer multiple times as my father fought his own battle with cancer. After my father was healed, we hardly had time to rest and recuperate before my mom's cancer came back. She passed away one week after their 33rd wedding anniversary at the age of 60. She was able to hear that my wife and I were expecting our fourth child, but she was never able to meet Sadie Ann, the little girl with the middle name after my mom.

After this point, my wife and I were taking care of four children under four years old while also grieving my mom and supporting my dad. If that wasn't enough, we were running a Mexican restaurant called Madres Mexican in our local mall. The same month we opened our restaurant, the church where I was employed told me they were in a difficult position financially and could no longer afford my salary. I held no ill will toward the church for making this decision, and I was thankful that we had spent the past year financially preparing to open the restaurant.

What we hadn't prepared for was a shooting in our mall that drove away many of our potential customers. When traffic finally started to return a year later, a group of 100 teenagers vandalized the mall and attacked many patrons in the process. Three months later, there was another shooting in the parking lot. Sales dropped to the point where I couldn't afford to pay myself after paying my employees.

My wife was working full time, but between our business expenses and our family obligations, we could hardly make ends meet. I vividly remember hard conversations about whether we should pay our bills on time or buy groceries so our family could eat. We felt broken, ashamed, and humiliated.

While this season was incredibly excruciating and painful, it was also a critical experience that taught me about what true faith in the Lord looks like. We felt like we had come to the end of ourselves, and prayer was our only lifeline. We had no option but to trust that God would provide for us, which is exactly what happened. God provided for us through a friend who bought three months' worth of groceries for us, including the exact special formula our youngest daughter needed. To be clear, this friend knew nothing of our situation, but she felt that God told her to help us. We were blessed through an unexpected credit of overpayment from our food supplier that gave us about a month's worth of free food. I remember finding a $10 bill in the freight elevator one day when I wasn't sure if I had enough gas to get home.

As I reflect on this time in my life, I'm reminded of how God provided for us in both the big things and the little things. I'm also encouraged as I think about how God was building my character and my trust in the middle of this storm. It's difficult to say I'm glad it happened because I don't ever want to go through something like that again. However, I am ultimately grateful for the lessons I learned through the process.

Perhaps you stand at a crossroads as you come to this book. Maybe you've recognized that the way you've lived your life up until this point isn't working, and something needs to change. You might find yourself questioning your purpose in the world and wondering if there's a greater way to live than what you've tried so far. I'm glad you're here, and I can't wait to share this message with you.

This book will walk you through several key elements of each person's lifelong pursuit. You'll learn about how to determine your life purpose, discover your core values, and set meaningful and actionable goals. We'll discuss how to maintain motivation for the long haul and build strong leadership skills. We'll even cover topics such as cultivating character, developing integrity, and building strong relationships.

Before we wrap up, I'll help you think through how you can lock in your learning from this book in a way that encourages sustainable and consistent development. Far too often, people waste their time reading books because the book doesn't produce an impact that lasts longer than a few weeks after they finish reading. I want this book to be different because I believe this message is critical for each person.

You'll quickly realize that my faith is the most important element of my life. My perspective on the value of The Never-Ending Pursuit is grounded in my belief that God is all-powerful and that Jesus came to Earth to live as a man, die on the cross for the sins of the world, and resurrect on the third day. Each chapter will include passages from Scripture and Biblical examples that show how these concepts we'll discuss can play out in real life.

Each chapter will also end with reflective questions and actionable prompts. In my opinion, questions drive thinking, and I want to do my part to connect the dots between the theories and strategies you'll read about in this book and the applications you may experience in your everyday life. After the final chapter, you'll also find a detailed workbook designed for small group discussions. This book can be a great resource to go through with a spouse, a few close friends, a team at work, or a small group at church.

As you get ready to join me on this journey, I encourage you to reflect on the following question: "Who am I becoming?" Think about your current values, habits, goals, and motivations. Each of these components plays a critical role in your overall development. If you want to make meaningful changes in your life, it starts with casting a compelling vision for the future and creating the necessary steps to help you get from where you are to where you want to go.

Let the words of Peter in 2 Peter 1:5-8 (NLT) prepare you to embark on a new Pursuit: "In view of all this, make every effort to respond to God's promises. Supplement your faith with a generous provision of moral excellence, and moral excellence with knowledge, and knowledge with self-control, and self-control with patient endurance, and patient endurance with godliness, and godliness with brotherly affection, and brotherly affection with love for everyone. The more you grow like this, the more productive and useful you will be in your knowledge of our Lord Jesus Christ."

With this in mind, strap in, buckle up and get ready for the quite literal adventure of a lifetime. Don't forget to enjoy the journey. After all, that's the entire point.

CHAPTER ONE: DETERMINE YOUR PURPOSE

Like everything in this book, determining your purpose is a process. It's not cut-and-dry. Ultimately, it looks different for every person. At the same time, the journey to figure out why God placed you on this Earth and what unique purpose God has led you to is just as rewarding as the calling itself.

It took me many years to figure out what I wanted to do with my life. I switched my major five times in college. I had no shortage of interests, but after taking a few courses, I quickly realized that I didn't want to spend the rest of my life being a physical therapist or a graphic designer.

To tell you the truth, I had no idea what I wanted except that I knew I wanted something. I could sense that my life had a greater purpose, but I was growing tired of spinning my wheels and feeling as though I lacked direction.

I remember my freshman year at LaRoche College in Pittsburgh like it was yesterday. I chose to major in graphic design because I was good at art. I even won several art awards in high school. However, I hated my classes and decided to leave and go back home after my first semester.

While this may sound like a major step back, it actually helped me discover my true motivation. After leaving college, I ended up in a missions internship in Garden Valley, TX. I discovered that I had a passion for having a positive impact, and I left that internship more encouraged than ever to pursue a purpose that existed beyond myself.

I tell you this story because I know that it's easy to grow frustrated or resentful when you can't identify your purpose in life. I've been there, and I imagine most people would say the same. You shouldn't feel shame or guilt if you don't have everything figured out, but you also shouldn't let this be a reason why you don't continue moving forward. Don't be afraid to take the first step, even if you aren't sure about the destination or the route ahead. Sometimes, motion is just as important as direction.

Now that you know the pursuit is a journey you will never finish, I hope you feel a sense of peace. Since progress is a better goal than perfection, you can find fulfillment in the gradual pursuit of personal development without feeling guilty or inadequate that you haven't "arrived" yet. The truth is, nobody has, and nobody ever will.

However, this doesn't mean we shouldn't have some sort of target. If you aim at nothing, you'll hit nothing. Without a clear sense of our purpose in life, we can easily lose focus, which is why we must begin this journey by identifying our purpose.

Whether you realize it or not, you're living with a purpose. Unfortunately, some people lack awareness of their purpose, and others live for a purpose too small or temporary to provide true meaning in life. Few things make me sadder than thinking about all the people who spent their lives chasing power, money, or prestige only to reach the end of their lives and find that they wasted their effort. They feel dissatisfied, and it's too late to go back and make any changes.

As a Christian, I believe that Jesus is the ultimate source of fulfillment for each person, and unless our purpose connects back to glorifying Jesus, we'll ultimately be dissatisfied. At the same time, if we can develop a strong understanding of our unique purpose in life, we'll position ourselves to make an impact that lives long after we're gone.

Think about the apostle Paul, who discovered his purpose in a powerful experience on the road to Damascus. When we first meet Paul (Saul before his name change) at the end of Acts 7, he's looking on as the members of the Sanhedrin stone Stephen, a man on trial and murdered based on a false charge that he was blaspheming against God (Acts 6:11).

Later, we learn that Paul was planning a trip to Damascus to bring new Christians back to Jerusalem as prisoners. While on the journey, Paul heard the voice of Jesus speaking as a bright light shone on his face. After this encounter, Paul was unable to see for three days. Jesus instructed him to finish the journey to Damascus and assured him that he would find out what he was supposed to do when he arrived.

Meanwhile, the Lord called a man named Ananias in Damascus and told him to go to Paul to heal him. As you can imagine, Paul had a reputation for being a dangerous threat to Christians, and Ananias felt uneasy about approaching Paul. Listen to God's response, taken directly from Acts 9:15-16 (NLT):

"But the Lord said, 'Go, for Saul is my chosen instrument to take my message to the Gentiles and to kings, as well as to the people of Israel. And I will show him how much he must suffer for my name's sake.' "

After this, Ananias met Paul, placed his hands on him, and restored his sight. It didn't take long before Paul began preaching that Jesus was the son of God. Paul spent the rest of his life proclaiming to the Gentiles that Jesus was the son of God. For the rest of Paul's life, nothing – not even the intense persecution and opposition he faced – could stop him from pursuing his purpose and calling.

I share this story for a few reasons. First of all, I've always appreciated how God was able to use Paul in such a powerful way. Initially, you could argue that Paul was the greatest threat to the early church based on his commitment to killing Christians. Regardless, God called Paul his "chosen instrument" and used Paul in an incredible way to spread the Gospel and develop the church.

More importantly, for the sake of this chapter, I believe Paul's story communicates a powerful truth about purpose. Purpose is dynamic - it's not identical for each person. While faith should play a critical role in your perception of your purpose, I want to challenge you to think more specifically and critically about why God has placed you on this Earth.

When we look back at Paul's story, we recognize that Paul had two unique, God-given purposes. Both are referenced in Acts 9:15-16:

- Proclaiming Jesus' name to the Gentiles, their kings, and the people of Israel.
- Suffering much in the name of Jesus.

So, why was this Paul's purpose? There are a number of factors that come into play. First and foremost, there was a great need in the world for somebody to bridge the gap between the Jews and Gentiles. Ironically, the man God chose for this task was somebody who spent the first part of his life as a devout Jew. Part of me thinks that God has a great sense of humor, and the other part believes that God chooses to work in ways that are incomprehensible and outrageous by human standards so that we have no other possible explanation for what's taking place outside of God's incredible power.

At the same time, let's think about what we know about Paul's personality even before his conversion on the road to Damascus. First of all, Paul was incredibly passionate. Paul briefly shares about his past in Philippians 3:5-6 (NLT):

> "I was circumcised when I was eight days old. I am a pure-blooded citizen of Israel and a member of the tribe of Benjamin—a real Hebrew if there ever was one! I was a member of the Pharisees, who demand the strictest obedience to the Jewish law. I was so zealous that I harshly persecuted the church. And as for righteousness, I obeyed the law without fault."

We often think about Pharisees in a negative light. This is because, in the Gospel narrative, the Pharisees are the antagonists. They oppose Jesus and eventually play a major role in facilitating His execution. However, Pharisees originated as a group devoted to the strictest upholding of the law. Although their intentions were initially good, their "righteous" deeds became misguided over time. They were deeply passionate and knowledgeable scholars who took their faith very seriously.

This depiction gives us some clues about the person Paul was. He knew the Torah. He valued his faith and worked hard to apply it in every area of his life. As a scholar, he was well-equipped to think about difficult concepts at a high level. When you think about how well Paul knew the Hebrew scriptures inside and out, you begin to understand how he was able to effectively incorporate the Hebrew scriptures into many of his New Testament letters.

By now, you're hopefully beginning to see how the world's needs and Paul's unique personality intersected in a powerful way to produce his God-given purpose. Frederick Buechner once said, "The place God calls you to is the place where your deep gladness and the world's deep hunger meet."

Like Paul, your purpose may lie at the intersection between your deepest passions and the world's current problems and issues. Furthermore, there's a good chance your unique passions, skills, and circumstances could provide clues about your purpose. Perhaps you've always enjoyed painting or drawing, so you decide your purpose is to reflect the glory of God in creation by crafting breathtaking pieces of art that depict the beauty of God's creation.

Each person's purpose is unique, and determining your purpose may take some time. However, it's an important process to experience, especially because of the significant advantages of clarifying your purpose. Here are a few benefits that you'll experience when you can clearly articulate your purpose – and when you're committed to living from your sense of purpose each day:

- **You can set strong goals for the future.** We can be more reactive to instantaneous concerns and urgent tasks when we think short-term. When we look toward the future, it's easier to plan based on what we want most.
- **You know when to say "yes" and when to say "no."** If you're living with a strong sense of your purpose, you can clearly decide what endeavors are worth your time and what opportunities are distractions.
- **You can develop resilience in adversity.** Living with purpose doesn't mean that your life will be perfect, but it does mean that you'll have an easier time staying focused and moving forward as you face challenges.
- **You can surround yourself with people who have similar values.** Since you often adopt the qualities and traits of the people around you, you can reinforce your purpose by forming relationships with people who share your values.

Ultimately, living out your purpose will give you a powerful sense of joy and the sense that you're following God's calling. You'll be amazed to see how God can work when you take a step of obedience and pursue the purpose God has determined for your life.

Perhaps you resonate with the idea of finding your calling in life, but you struggle with knowing where to start. While clarifying your purpose can certainly take some work, it's a worthwhile endeavor to help you envision how to find more fulfillment and meaning in life. As you begin to understand your purpose, you'll also position yourself to make a greater impact on your family and community.

With this in mind, I'd love to help you think about what your unique purpose could be. Here are five questions that may give you ideas or spur your imagination:

- **How do I want people to remember me?** Think about what your friends and family may say at your funeral. What sort of legacy do you want to leave behind? This may reveal clues about your purpose or calling in life.
- **If I could wave a magic wand and fix one problem in the world, what would that be?** Remember, purpose can come at the intersection between your passion and the world's needs. So, what keeps you up at night? What injustice or inadequacy makes you feel physically sick to your stomach?
- **What gives me energy?** What could you do for hours and never get bored or tired? Each person is built differently, and identifying what naturally

brings you joy can easily provide clues about your calling.

- **What do I do better than 90% of people in the world?** Proficiency or natural aptitude can also reveal your purpose. There's a chance that God blessed you with unique skills and abilities to point you toward your calling.
- **If money was no object, how would I spend my time?** Imagine that you would make the same amount of money regardless of your job. What kind of work would you choose to do? When you remove money from the equation, you measure success with different metrics (fulfillment, impact, etc.), and you better understand your values and passions.
- **If I wasn't afraid of anything, what would I do?** God may call you to something that scares you, but He'll also provide you with the strength you need. As we live out our calling despite our fear, our relationship with God grows stronger as we deepen our reliance on God.

Some people may feel fear as they start to think about their purpose or calling on a deeper level. This is your brain's natural response to unfamiliar situations. However, you'll likely have to overcome fear and step out in faith if you're going to pursue God's purpose or calling in your life. Remember the words of Paul in 2 Timothy 1:7 (NKJV) "For God has not given us a spirit of fear, but of power and of love and of a sound mind."

Sometimes, the journey to abandon fear and trust in God's power is a pursuit in itself. If you need further proof, look no further than the story of Gideon. When we meet Gideon in Judges 6, he's threshing wheat at the bottom of a winepress so that the Midianites won't find his grain. Usually, wheat threshing happens in an open-air elevated area so that the wind can blow away the chaff. However, Gideon was afraid of the Midianites, so he took a non-conventional approach. His unique circumstances reflected the strange position the Israelites were in at the time. They were oppressed and struggling to survive under Midianite rule.

God's angel approached Gideon in this situation with a powerful declaration - "Mighty hero, the Lord is with you!" I love the irony of this moment. Gideon may be threshing wheat in a pit, but in God's eyes, he is a mighty warrior. Of course, Gideon didn't see himself this way. He pushed back on the angel's claim and even questioned God's sovereignty in the midst of their situation. " 'Sir,' Gideon replied, 'if the Lord is with us, why has all this happened to us?' " (Judges 6:13, NLT) He even accuses God of abandoning them and giving them to their enemies.

God responds by assuring Gideon that the time for redemption is here. God tells Gideon that he will be the one to rescue Israel from Midian's hand. Although God is the one commissioning Gideon to take action, God also acknowledges the strength that Gideon brings to the table. Keep this detail in mind - it's going to come back into play later.

Once again, Gideon isn't quite on board with this plan. He questions whether he has the ability to rescue Israel based on his low position within his family and his traditionally weak community. God's encouragement is simple. God doesn't attempt to talk Gideon out of his feelings. God doesn't assure Gideon that he's better than he thinks. All God says is, "I will be with you."

As we make our way on the pursuit that is our lives, let us never forget this powerful truth. No matter where we go or what hand we're dealt, God is always with us. As God told Joshua in Joshua 1:9, we can be strong and courageous because we remember that God is with us through each step.

If you're reading this sentence right now, you're called to a unique purpose. God has gifted you with special traits and qualities that you can use to make an impact on the world. When God encourages Gideon, He doesn't only remind Gideon of His presence. He also instructs Gideon to focus on His own strengths. He helps Gideon see that he's equipped for the task at hand, even if he doesn't notice his own capabilities.

I don't say this to make Gideon out to be more of a hero than he really was (although to be fair, God Himself called Gideon a hero). I say this because, like you and me, Gideon was created with God-given strengths and capabilities that aligned with the purpose God had designed for his life. God, in His foreknowledge, knew that Gideon would one day be in a position to lead Israel out of Midianite oppression and created Gideon with the gifts and strengths necessary to do the job well.

You might still be figuring out what your gifts are, and you may not have full clarity about the road ahead. Let me encourage you to move forward anyway. Don't be afraid to take the first step and get in motion. God is with you every step of the way, and He is bigger than every one of your fears. Once you have a sense of God's purpose and calling for your life, I expect you'll also begin to see how God created you with specific attributes to serve you well as you pursue the purpose God chose for you.

As you think about how to apply this chapter, spend time in prayer, asking for wisdom and clarity around the purpose God has chosen for your life. Ask for wisdom and clarity as you look for opportunities to use your gifts and serve the people around you. Your relationship with God will grow as you think about the plans God has for your life.

Application Questions

1. How much clarity do you currently have about your life's purpose? What questions do you still have?
2. Which of the five questions from earlier in the chapter about identifying your purpose was most thought-provoking or meaningful to you?
3. What's keeping you from fully living from your sense of purpose? Is it fear, uncertainty, or something else?
4. What's one step you can take to better live out your purpose?

CHAPTER TWO: DEFINING YOUR CORE VALUES

If you've ever flown with Southwest Airlines, you know that they function quite differently from any other major airliner. For starters, they don't assign seats. Once you board the plane, seating is open, and you can choose whatever position on the plane you want. Unless you're flying with a young child and they demand the window seat and relegate you to the middle seat (I may or may not be speaking from experience here).

Another major difference with Southwest is the relaxed demeanor of many of their crew members. It's not uncommon for flight attendants to make jokes during the safety instruction process or for the pilots to mix in a dose of humor or self-deprecation to their otherwise routine flight updates.

Many customers enjoy this fresh take on air travel, but some don't. In fact, one specific customer decided she'd had enough. She began writing complaints to Southwest after each flight. She was frustrated at the lack of seat assignments, the absence of in-flight meals, and her inability to sit in first class because Southwest didn't provide different classes of seats.

Just to be clear - she didn't write only one letter. In fact, she became famous within Southwest's customer service department, with some team members even beginning to call her "Pen Pal." However, over time, the representatives struggled to provide responses to her ongoing correspondence and eventually brought a letter to Herb Keller, Southwest's CEO at the time. Herb decided to write back to this customer himself and penned a short response in less than sixty seconds:

"Dear Ms. Crabapple,

We will miss you.

Love, Herb."

I love this story because it shows what makes Southwest Airlines unique. They know who they are, and they know what they are not. More importantly, they have determined that humility and friendliness are among their top values, and they are willing to see customers walk away if those traits don't align with what they are looking for from their airline. I also wonder why this woman continued to fly Southwest if she had so many issues with them, but that's a conversation for another day.

Whether you're a major national airliner or a person trying to live out their Never-Ending Pursuit, knowing your core values is essential. Your core values will impact not only what you do but how you do it. Whenever I'm onboarding a new team member at the restaurant, I always recite our restaurant's "Ultra-Purpose." Although it may surprise you, it has very little to do with how to make chicken sandwiches, prepare customers' orders, or mix delicious milkshakes (I'll never reveal our secret).

It's not that I don't think these things are important. Obviously, I own and operate a restaurant, and people wouldn't show up if we didn't feed them. However, at my Chick-fil-A[1], we care about much more than serving delicious chicken. Although we think our food is fantastic, we exist for something greater.

If you've never visited the Chick-fil-A company values page, I encourage you to check it out. You'll learn why the restaurants are Closed on Sundays and what they care about most as an organization. You'll discover the foundational purpose of Chick-fil-A: "To glorify God by being a faithful steward of all that is entrusted to us and to have a positive influence on all who come in contact with Chick-fil-A." You'll hear more about the Chick-fil-A commitment to creating a culture of belonging by including people from unique backgrounds and experiences. You'll even read some of the company's thoughts on innovation and how it's reflected in everything from a commitment to upcycling and efforts to create parent-friendly menus.

In short, you'll quickly find that Chick-fil-A is built on a strong purpose and a clear set of values. We spent the first chapter discussing the importance of purpose and how that impacts our pursuits in life. Values and purpose go hand-in-hand with each other, although they are not the same thing.

To put it simply, if you tell me your purpose, I'll know what you're trying to accomplish. If you tell me your values, I'll know what you care about. I could deduce what you care

---

[1] https://www.chick-fil-a.com/about/who-we-are

about from hearing your purpose, and I may infer what your purpose is if you tell me your values. Again, values and purpose are deeply connected, even if they aren't identical.

Chick-fil-A values diversity, inclusion, family, community engagement, and innovation, among other things. Each value connects back to the organization's greater purpose. I recognize that these words can stir up a wide range of emotions in today's world. To me, these words are simply communicating care and concern for everyone who walks through the doors. They strive to treat all people with honor, dignity, and respect because they are human beings made in the image of God.

As a Chick-fil-A owner, I care deeply about infusing these values into the work of my local franchise. It's what led me to start the "Pursuit" blog[2] on our restaurant's Grow University website. It's what motivates me to provide free college tuition for team members. It's why our restaurant has donated over $750,000 to our community in food donations and support, along with $150,000 in food donations to our local homeless shelters. That's just up until the writing of this book - these numbers should continue to grow in the future.

All these contributions and initiatives connect back to our store's ultra-purpose: "We're not only here to sell chicken. We're here to make a difference in the lives of every team member and guest. When people become our focus, we'll sell more chicken than we could ever imagine."

---

[2] https://growuniversitychickfila.com/blog

As a Chick-fil-A owner/operator, my top values are service, intentionality, and going the extra mile. I want to make a difference in the lives of each person who eats at our restaurant. I want team members who are willing to take their efforts to the next level because of their love for people. I believe that if we do this well, we'll sell more than enough chicken.

Ultimately, the desire to improve our local community gets me out of bed in the morning. I believe I'm not in the chicken business but in the people business.[3] I told you in the introduction about the time I spent as a youth pastor at a small church in Pennsylvania. Although I no longer work in traditional full-time church ministry, I see myself doing ministry every day by serving our guests and team members.

You can see how my purpose and my values impact the work I do each day in our restaurant. Because I value people, I approach business much differently than if I were more concerned about profit or growth. There's nothing wrong with those things; in fact, you need profit and growth to have a healthy business. We aren't a non-profit charity, and we're able to better invest in people as profits grow. At the same time, from my perspective, people take precedence. And this perception impacts everything I do.

Identifying your core values can be an incredibly powerful exercise. When you understand what you care about and what drives you to do what you'll do, you'll be able to

---

[3] https://growuniversitychickfila.com/people-not-chicken

make intentional choices about how you spend your time and where you direct your focus.

If you've never spent time thinking about your core values, I would encourage you to reflect on the traits and qualities most important to you. Think about what goals and outcomes you're willing to make sacrifices to achieve. Consider how you spend your time and money and what it says about what you truly care about. Ask others what they would identify as your core values based on what they know about you.

Most importantly, remember that you aren't confined by where you currently stand. This is a foundational truth about "The Never-Ending Pursuit". You don't have to stay where you are. You have all the power to move forward, but unless you identify where you want to go, you will continue to wander aimlessly. On the other hand, once you begin to do the work and uncover what's already there and what could improve, you'll begin to realize that you control your values more than you think.

I appreciate the way Patrick Lencioni talks about values in his best-selling book "The Advantage." Although he is mainly speaking about organizational values, I believe these teachings can apply to individuals as well. According to Lencioni, there are four main types of values:

- **Aspirational values.** These are the values that you don't currently have but would like to have one day. For example, if you're not good at managing money but would like to be better at saving and budgeting, stewardship might be an aspirational value.

- **Permission-to-play values.** These represent the minimum standards based on your situation or community, but they don't make you different or unique. In other words, regularly showering and brushing your teeth doesn't necessarily mean that you value hygiene - it's something everyone does.
- **Accidental values.** Accidental values are the ones you stumble into unintentionally, and they may or may not serve a purpose. It's the person who grows so accustomed to stopping for coffee on their way to work that their morning drive-thru coffee trip accidentally becomes one of their values.
- **Core values.** Core values are the 3-4 attributes and qualities most important to us. They align with our purpose, and they are connected to our passions and goals.

One lesson I take from this framework is that not all values are created equally. The value I see in caring for my family (which I would categorize as a core value) is different from the accidental value I see in mixing Chick-fil-A and Buffalo sauce.[4]

Another takeaway is that different values are created in different ways. Some values are created accidentally. Other values, such as permission-to-play values, are influenced by our surroundings. But what about core

---

[4] Seriously, it's the best sauce combination. Give it a try.

values? Where do those come from, and how much control do we have over what we value most?

As children, we're taught about meaning and significance. Our parents are our primary examples, but we also pick up quite a bit from teachers, coaches, other adults, friends, and society. We may go through a personal experience that impacts the way we see the world and what we perceive as important.

While there are many sources that can contribute to our values, they share one commonality: they come from external sources. This means that without personal reflection and contemplation, we can allow others to choose our values for us. We must be willing to spend the time and energy necessary to think deeply about what's most important to us and how we can live a life based on our top values.

As we continue to think about core values, let's examine some of Jesus' core values by looking at a few stories from His life. You'll quickly see how you can identify what somebody cares about by listening to their words and watching their actions.

- **Integrity.** All four Gospel accounts tell the story of Jesus' temptation in the wilderness. During this time, He's tested by Satan on multiple occasions, but He doesn't respond to the devil's requests. (see Matthew 4) This story also shows us how Jesus values perseverance, growth in struggles, and faith that God will provide in the hardest situations.

- **Forgiveness.** Jesus spent much time healing people of various diseases and conditions. Since the common belief at the time was that physical conditions were a consequence of sin, Jesus' miraculous healings show us how He valued forgiveness and reconciliation. (See Matthew 4:23-25, 8:1-7)
- **Humility.** Jesus spoke on many occasions about reversing the traditional order of society. He encouraged His disciples to accept low positions with little honor, knowing that God would exalt those who were willing to humble themselves. He also put children in a position of prominence and encouraged His followers to adopt a similar position (see Matthew 11 and 18).
- **Inclusion.** Jesus welcomed and accepted the Gentiles, a group of people who had long been excluded by Jewish religious leaders. He spent time teaching and healing Gentile people during His Earthly ministry. While Jesus was for everyone, He loved them too much to remain as they were and called them to become like Him. (see Matthew 15).
- **Service.** The commitment to serve others is a natural application of the value of humility. When you elevate the needs of others at the expense of your own, you're driven to serve others in the same way that Jesus did (see Matthew 20:26-28)
- **Sacrifice.** If a core value is something you're willing to sacrifice for, there's no greater sacrifice than what Jesus did for you and me on the cross. Through Jesus' death and resurrection, we learn

that God values mercy, forgiveness, and the salvation of each person who puts their trust in Jesus.

Through Jesus' life and ministry, we gain a clear picture of what traits and qualities He values. As His disciples, we're called to emulate His attitude and practices in the way we live our lives. If Jesus valued attributes such as integrity, forgiveness, humility, inclusion, service, and sacrifice, it's only logical that we, as Christ-followers, should follow suit.

There will come times when you feel tempted to abandon your core values and react to what's happening at the moment. Life is hard. Trust me, I've experienced my fair share of struggles and obstacles. Although I'm far from perfect myself, I believe that times of adversity are the exact moments when you must make decisions based on your top values.

One of my favorite stories in the entire Bible is the story of Joseph. Joseph was one of Jacob's twelve sons and his first son with Rachel, the woman he instantly fell in love with after the first time he saw her. Because of this, Jacob favored Joseph and gifted him a special coat to symbolize his affection (see Genesis 37:3).

As you can imagine, Joseph's brothers were jealous of the preferential treatment he received from their father. To make matters worse, Joseph shared openly about his dreams, where he would one day rule over his brothers and his father. Because of their jealousy, Joseph's brothers devised a plan to take his life. Ultimately, they chose to sell him into Egyptian slavery instead of murdering him (but they told Jacob that a wild animal devoured him).

You probably know what happens next if you've heard this story before. However, let's pause to consider a question. What would you have done in this situation? Would you have fallen into perpetual cynicism? Would you become convinced the world was horrible, and everyone was out to get you? Would you become filled with vengeance and the desire to pursue revenge?

I love this story because Joseph's response was not what anybody would expect. Joseph responded with faith and integrity rather than carrying a grudge against his brothers. He responded to his situation with purpose and conviction rather than reacting out of anger or frustration.

Once he arrived in Egypt, he became a slave in the house of Potiphar, a high-ranking Egyptian official. Potipher was impressed with Joseph and entrusted Joseph with everything in his house. However, the relationship ended poorly when Potipher's wife lied to her husband and said that Joseph tried to seduce her. This false claim unfairly landed Joseph in prison, where he again found favor in the eyes of the individuals in charge because of his character and diligence.

Ultimately, Joseph rose to power in Egypt. He was released from slavery and made second-in-command to Pharaoh. He reconciled with his brothers and even saw his father again during his reign. Although his story ends on a high note, it doesn't eliminate the struggles and obstacles he faced throughout his life. At the same time, that's not the point.

As we bring this story home and consider what it means today, we must remember that obstacles are inevitable. My own pastor has preached, "We're either in a storm, coming out of a storm, or about to go into one." What matters is not if we experience obstacles but how we respond when we face adversity.

The ability to persevere through hard times is a key component of The Never-Ending Pursuit, and it's what stands out to me from Joseph's life. Joseph didn't allow his struggles to defeat him or compromise his values. Instead, Joseph shined brightest when the odds were stacked against him. He leaned into his faith and character despite what was happening around him.

As Joseph reflected on his journey at the end of his life, he shared a powerful message with his brothers. He acknowledged that they intended to harm him through their actions, but he reminded them of how God chose to use the situation for good.

Joseph's declaration is a powerful perspective on God's incredible redemptive power. At the same time, it's an invitation to see God's hand in all seasons of life - the good, the bad, and the ugly. It reminds us to live out our core values and faith, even when faced with adversity. Finally, it's an encouragement that we may not know what lies ahead, but God is always in control, and God will work in mysterious ways when we step back and allow Him to lead our lives.

As we wrap up this chapter and try to make these teachings practical, it's important to acknowledge that we all find ourselves at different points on the journey. Some people will have a clear understanding of their top values and what it looks like to put these values into practice. Others may still be going through the process of naming their values, and some people might lack clarity about how to live out their values in a meaningful way.

Like everything in this book, living from your values is a journey. It's not something you'll ever finish or complete, and you can't check it off your list. However, there's always an opportunity to move forward. One of my favorite questions is, "What's a step that's big enough to make a difference but small enough to have an impact?" We'll talk more about this one later, but for now, consider this question as you think about how to identify and practice your values on a more consistent basis. What could you realistically do today that would make a meaningful impact?

Application questions

1. Think about how you spend your time and money. What does this say about your values?
2. What's the gap between your aspirational values and your actual values? How can you close this gap?
3. Think about the list of Jesus' core values. Which value is easiest for you to exemplify? Which one is the hardest?

CHAPTER THREE:
SETTING MEANINGFUL GOALS

Since we moved to Iowa, my youngest daughter has become obsessed with gymnastics. To be honest with you, her dedication is quite admirable. She's willing to spend hours practicing and training at the gym, even if it means repeatedly going over the same motions. Then, she'll come home and immediately start working on her trampoline or balance beam after she walks through the door.

I get tired just thinking about the amount of time and energy she's willing to invest in perfecting her routine. I don't know many people who could spend six hours at organized practice only to come home and immediately start working independently!

What's even more amazing is the fact that she didn't compete in her first event until several years after she began training. While that may be shocking to hear, it is actually quite normal for most high-level gymnasts. They must practice the basic movements until they achieve the point of mastery where they can complete these actions unconsciously. The more my daughter (or any other gymnast) practices her skills, the more natural or habitual they become.

The last skill my daughter had to learn before she could compete on the Junior Olympics team was a move called the "kip." If you've ever watched high-level gymnasts on TV during the summer Olympics, you've probably seen the kip without realizing what was happening. When performing the kip, a gymnast jumps to grab the low bar and swings their body underneath with their arms extended while pulling themselves up above the bar. When they finish, they hold themselves up high while resting their waist on the bar in front of them.

Although skilled athletes make the kip look effortless and easy, it's actually very challenging. All Gold Medal winners, at some point, spent several months working to master this move, and my daughter was no exception. She spent several months training without any results. She expressed feelings of frustration and discouragement when speaking with her mom and me. At times, she thought she would never be able to perform the kip, but she didn't stop trying.

One day, during our family prayer time, she asked God for wisdom to be able to perform the kip. To our amazement, she did the kip for the first time a few days later and has been able to do it easily every time since. It may look natural to spectators who are watching her compete for the first time (and it may not seem like a move that requires advanced skill), but I know how hard she worked to master that move.

I take a few key lessons away from this story. First of all, we should never underestimate the power of prayer or God's ability to do for us what we can't do for ourselves. I once heard somebody say that we should leave nothing up to chance, but we should leave room for God to work. I believe that's what my daughter did in this situation. She controlled what was within her power while recognizing that God's provision would be the force that pushed her over the top.

In addition, we have to remember that achieving our goals takes hard work. We live in a world where you can become an overnight success by going viral on YouTube. While this is true for .001 percent of people, most of us have to work hard and persevere for years to experience true success. This is hard to accept in a world where we have same-day Amazon delivery and 5G cell phone service that loads our favorite web pages and apps in a split second. However, when we remember that true joy in life comes from the pursuit and not only from arriving at a particular destination, this reminder is actually quite encouraging.

Once you get a clear picture of your values and your purpose, you can begin to make these concepts actionable in the form of clear and captivating goals. I've always had a personal fascination with goals. Setting goals allows you to create your ideal future while offering your current self a greater sense of purpose and direction.

Think about it this way - if life is a pursuit, the goals are the stops you plan to take along the way. They aren't ends in themselves, but they are checkpoints or milestones on the route to your ultimate destination.

Perhaps you're interested in working toward one or more goals, but you aren't sure how to choose these goals. Let's dive into a few questions that will help you consider what goals you could set and what value they might have for you.

Question One: What do you want to be true?

As I consider what I want to happen in my life in the coming months and years, I can work backward to create the necessary steps to help me get where I want to go. This simple exercise is incredibly powerful, and I encourage you to set aside some time to go down this creative rabbit trail, especially if you've never envisioned your preferred future.

Let's start right now. Imagine your ideal self. What are you doing? What are you accomplishing? More importantly, who are you becoming? Whether you envision the short-term (3-6 months) or long-term (5-10 years), this can be a great way to identify potential goals.

We can make this even more practical by envisioning our lives in specific domains. Perhaps you're familiar with Zig Ziglar's "Wheel of Life." Ziglar believed our lives were like wheels, with specific areas representing different spokes on the wheel. From Ziglar's perspective, the only way to live a complete and well-rounded life was to focus attention on each component of our life.

Ziglar's "Wheel of Life" had seven spokes:

- **Spiritual.** How is your relationship with God? Are you living out your faith on a daily basis?

- **Physical.** How is your physical health and well-being? Are you regularly exercising, eating healthy meals, and taking care of yourself?
- **Mental.** How is your mental health? Are you finding opportunities to learn through reading books or taking classes?
- **Personal.** Are you feeling personally fulfilled and satisfied? Are you setting meaningful goals, participating in hobbies that bring you joy, and feeling satisfied with your current context and community?
- **Family.** How are your relationships with family, friends, and other loved ones? Do you have close relationships with people who support and value you?
- **Financial.** Are you being a good steward with the financial resources that you have? Are you able to pay your bills while saving and investing in your future?
- **Career.** How satisfied are you with your current job? Are you taking steps to grow your career and further your impact?

As you read through each of these categories, you probably identified one or two domains where you feel some degree of tension or dissatisfaction. Perhaps these are the areas where you need to set some goals for the future. Envision what you want to be true in these domains, and create goals that will help you get where you want to go.

Question Two: What's holding you back?

As you think about what you want the future to look like, you may also begin to recognize the gap that exists between where you are and where you want to be. Initially, seeing the gap can be discouraging. However, once you notice it exists, you also begin to generate ideas for potential goals that can help you bridge that gap.

For example, say you want to run a marathon, but you're not happy with your current diet. Your initial goal could be to log your calories each day or limit yourself to one cheat meal or dessert each week. If you want to start a side hustle but don't currently have any money in savings, your first goal may be to set aside $1,000 of extra funds to help you get your new business off the ground.

This perspective is hard for me to adopt because of my desire to see instantaneous results. If I were the one at her age training to be a gymnast and not my daughter, I probably would have given up on the kip after a few weeks. I have since learned that progress takes time.

A question that helps me reframe my expectation for instant gratification is, "What's a step that's big enough to make an impact but small enough to be doable?" I love this question because it forces us to think about our long-term aspirations along with attainable short-term progress. It enables us to see opportunities to make small changes that can produce a massive difference in the long term. These subtle shifts may not seem significant initially, but if you commit to consistency, you'll be surprised at how one small daily change can produce a massive long-term impact.

Question Three: What would make a difference?

Most of us will feel the natural temptation to think primarily about our own lives when answering the first question ("What do you want to be true?"). While this is understandable, our goals should focus on elevating others' lives and not only our own.

When I think about a person who sets goals based on their desire to serve others, I immediately think about Jesus. Jesus is the perfect embodiment of each of the concepts in this book, but His example is especially relevant here.

In Luke 19, Jesus is making His way through Jericho. Word traveled quickly around the town that He was passing through, and large crowds came out to catch a glimpse of Jesus and His disciples. A local man named Zacchaeus was one of many who came out to see Jesus, but he wasn't able to see over the crowds because he was a wee little man (and a wee little man was he. Come on, I had to work in everyone's favorite VBS song somehow).

Zacchaeus's lack of height wasn't the only factor working against him. Zacchaeus was also a chief tax collector. In the first-century Greco-Roman world, tax collectors were known for exploiting the tax system for their own personal gain. They would often charge people more than what they owed and keep the profits for themselves. Although many tax collectors were Jews, they were working in tandem with the Roman government, and many of their fellow Jews looked at them as traitors.

Zacchaeus was not only a tax collector but a chief tax collector. This likely meant that he had worked for so long as a tax collector that he had achieved notable wealth and influence, especially in the Roman government. In other words, Zacchaeus had probably been overcharging people for years and was so good at his job that the Romans gave him a promotion.

Despite his colorful past, Zacchaeus was interested in seeing Jesus when He came through town. He quickly realized that he had no shot of seeing Jesus over the crowd - both because of his lack of physical height as well as the lack of motivation for any of his fellow countrymen to make way so that he could come through. At the same time, Zacchaeus was creative and innovative, and he came up with another idea for how he could see Jesus. He spots a tree near the path where Jesus would be walking and climbs up into its branches so that he can see Jesus come by.

Let's pause here to consider the absurdity of what's taking place. We have a wealthy man with multiple direct reports and a reputation within the local government climbing a tree so that he can catch a quick glimpse of another man who's out on a stroll with His friends. I can't help but wonder what others would have thought when they saw Zaccheaus putting himself in this position, but his intentions were clear. For whatever reason, Zacchaeus wanted to see Jesus.

More importantly, Jesus wanted to see Zacchaeus. Jesus spots Zacchaeus in the tree and offers him an invitation. "Zacchaeus! Quick, come down! I must be a guest in your house today." The crowds were immediately taken aback. *Why would Jesus want to spend time with this man? Does He not understand what he's done to us? Does He even care about all he's taken from me and my family?*

Something about receiving attention from Jesus Himself immediately transformed Zacchaeus's heart and mind. In front of everybody, Zacchaeus makes a promise to be a different man going forward. Not only will he give half of all he owns to the poor, but he will also pay back four times the amount that he's cheated anyone on their taxes. Not only is Zacchaeus making amends for past wrongdoing, but he's adopting a new identity. His life will no longer be about wealth and prosperity at others' expense. From this point on, Zacchaeus's life would be about elevating the needs of others and embodying values such as honesty and service.

Jesus responds to this awesome declaration by proclaiming that Zacchaeus has experienced salvation and by reminding all who were in attendance that His goal was to "seek and save those who are lost" (Luke 19:10, NLT). This wasn't just a passion project for Jesus, but it was the entire reason why He came into the world to live as a man in the first place. Jesus didn't just pursue this goal by walking through random towns and looking for tax collectors in trees. He achieved this goal by picking up a tree on His own, carrying it to Calvary, and giving His life in a gruesome manner for each sinner who has ever lived. Yes, that includes both you and me.

I tell this story because it's one of my favorites in the entire Bible and because I see Jesus perfectly encapsulating the marriage of a clear purpose, strong values, and well-defined goals. Jesus' purpose, as He proclaimed to Zacchaeus and the crowd in Verse 10, was to seek and save the lost. From this assertion, we learn that Jesus values pursuing sinners, making Himself known to them, forgiving them of their sins, and allowing them to experience grace and salvation.

Jesus' purpose and values manifest themselves in the practical application of going through towns, identifying people who are lost, building relationships with them, and showing them a better way of life. Jesus' goals weren't about furthering His own interests or desires but about advancing and elevating the status of others who had been overlooked or marginalized in society.

Here's my question - what if we had the same mindset? What if we thought about potential goals not only for the value that they could bring to our lives but for the ways that they could benefit others in our families, social circles, churches, workplaces, and community? What if we became known as people who cared deeply about using our talents, interests, and resources to improve the position of others? What if being the hands and feet of Jesus was our primary pursuit, and what if this became something that we could apply to our daily lives through the goals that we set?

How to Set Powerful Goals

By now, you can tell that I'm a big fan of goals. However, I also believe that not all goals are created equally. In order to set goals that motivate us to take action, we must learn how to set the right goals. This takes more time and energy on the front end, but it's the best way to ensure that we're able to reap the greatest benefit from working on (and completing) our goals.

Perhaps you're familiar with the SMART acronym and how it relates to goal-setting. Here's a basic breakdown of what it means to make a goal SMART. SMART goals must meet each of the following criteria:

- **Specific.** Setting specific goals will help you clarify what you want to accomplish so that you aren't confused about the outcome you desire and what work you must do to accomplish your goal.
- **Measured.** Your goal should be measurable so that you can track your progress and understand whether or not you have achieved your goal.
- **Actionable.** Your goal should strike a balance between being challenging enough to stretch you and being easy enough to accomplish within a reasonable timeframe.
- **Results-oriented.** You shouldn't choose goals randomly, and you shouldn't waste your time on goals that don't connect to your larger purpose or objectives in life.
- **Time-bound.** Without a deadline, it can be easy to procrastinate. Aim to complete your goal by a certain time, and you'll feel a greater sense of urgency to start (or continue) working.

It's also crucial that you avoid some of the most common goal-setting mistakes. Don't fall into the trap of thinking that you'll reach a goal just because you identify a desirable outcome. If you're like me, you may sometimes enjoy setting goals more than actually pursuing them. Setting a goal can be exhilarating - after all, when you choose a goal, you instinctively think about how it will feel to accomplish the goal. You may even tell a friend about what you're planning, which enhances your excitement.

However, the hard part (doing the work necessary to achieve the goal) comes next. The initial rush of choosing a goal is quickly replaced with feelings of uncertainty about the process and the discomfort of doing hard and unfamiliar tasks. If you don't carefully approach the process of setting goals and planning for how you'll accomplish them, you'll be more likely to prematurely quit your goals and leave your potential unfulfilled.

To help you better prepare to achieve your goals, I'd like to share five common mistakes people often make when initially choosing their goals:

- **Thinking too big.** If your goal is too big, you may get discouraged if you don't feel like you're making progress. The idea of shooting for the moon and landing among the stars is only partially valid, as we'll discuss below.
- **Thinking too small.** You don't want your goal to be too big, but you also don't want to choose a goal that doesn't stretch or challenge you. They won't motivate you in the same way, and they won't help you reach your fullest potential.
- **Ignoring obstacles.** Ignoring obstacles on the path to reaching your goals won't make them go away. Consider beforehand what challenges you might face along the way, and make plans in advance for how you'll approach potential issues.
- **Ignoring progress.** One of the biggest mistakes high achievers make is failing to take time to

celebrate their progress. Not only does this reinforce how far you've already come, but it also gives you extra motivation to continue moving forward.

- **Expecting perfection.** Completing a goal is not a linear process. You'll have to figure out how to move past your mistakes and overcome various setbacks if you're ever going to achieve your goals. Don't beat yourself up for not being perfect. Instead, recognize that it's an essential part of the process and look for ways to continue moving forward even if things don't go according to your original plans.

I'll also offer a bonus idea here. One of my current favorite books is "Atomic Habits" by James Clear. In this book, Clear argues that winners and losers both have the same goals and that focusing on systems (rather than goals) is the best way to ensure continued progress and development. In other words, you're better off focusing on the daily actions or systems that will help you achieve your goals rather than focusing intensely on the goal itself. This will make your goal seem more attainable, and it will ensure that you're always making continued progress (however small it is).

Now that you know how to identify the right goals, make them SMART, and avoid the most common pitfalls, you're almost ready to begin choosing a few new goals for yourself. Before we wrap this chapter up, let me offer up one more piece of advice for you to bring along on your goal-setting journey.

Can Failed Goals Be a Good Thing?

There's a popular saying that reads, "Shoot for the moon. Even if you miss, you'll land among the stars." I remember reading this quote on a poster in one of my middle school math classes, but I didn't know anything about its origins until recently.

The quote was first attributed to Norman Vincent Peale, an author and pastor who lived and worked in the mid-1900s. Peale is well-known for his best-selling book, *The Power of Positive Thinking*.[5] Essentially, Peale wanted people to dream big and aim high because the outcome would still be positive even if they didn't reach their ultimate standards or aspirations.

I have mixed feelings about this quote. As we discussed above, I think one of the most critical mistakes people make when setting goals is choosing a goal that's too big. At the same time, I think there's tremendous value in Peale's perspective. I've always been taught to dream so big it scares me. This way, I know that God has to help, and I give Him glory when I achieve success because there's no other possible explanation for what takes place.

In addition, I believe a goal can serve you even if you ultimately fall short if it inspires you to take action. Let's say that you want to read more often. You aren't currently reading at all, so you set a goal to read twenty books in one year. Because you set the goal, you start

---

[5] https://www.amazon.com/Power-Positive-Thinking-Norman-Vincent/dp/0743234804

reading a few pages each day, and at the end of the year, you've read ten books.

So, was your goal a success? In one sense, you failed because you didn't reach your goal of twenty books. At the same time, you read more than you would have otherwise because of the goal you set. This means that your goal was a success.

We also must remember that our goals work for us, and we don't work for our goals. Imagine that you begin the year with the goal of reading twenty books, but during the year, your spouse or child is diagnosed with a serious health condition. Should you spend your free time caring for your loved one or pursuing your goal of reading twenty books? The answer is obvious, and this case study reminds us that we must account for circumstances outside of our control when we think about setting goals.

At the heart of this conversation is the idea that there's greater value to be found in setting goals than simply reaching (or not reaching) the goal. As you think about setting goals, I want to challenge you to get intensely curious about the outcome you desire from your goals. Ask questions like, what impact will working on this goal have on my life? How will it help me grow or develop, even if I don't ultimately achieve the goal? What am I willing to sacrifice in order to reach the goal, and what would it take for me to pause the goal or drop it entirely?

Considering these questions will reinforce that failed goals can still have a positive impact, and they will remind you that sometimes quitting a goal is actually the smartest thing you can do. Finally, as with everything else in this book, this perspective reinforces the idea that the journey - and not just the destination - is where we experience the full joy and richness of life.

Ready, Aim, Fire

Since we're majoring in slightly cliched sayings in this chapter, let me close with one more. "If you aim at nothing, you'll hit nothing." While this may seem like common sense, it's important to bring it up as we close our discussion on goal-setting.

Perhaps aiming at the moon isn't always the right answer, but firing without a target isn't wise either. Before you choose a goal, make sure it aligns with your purpose and your values. This will enhance your sense of urgency to make progress, and it will give you a greater sense of satisfaction when you eventually achieve the goal.

In the first three chapters, we've set an important foundation for the future ahead. We've discussed our purpose, our values, and our goals. The following chapter is crucial because we're going to begin to discuss the fuel that will move us from where we are to where we want to go. Without this piece of the puzzle, nothing is possible.

Application Questions

- Imagine your life in five years. What do you want to be true?
- Think about a time when you achieved a big goal. What can you take away from that experience that

might be helpful as you think about pursuing future goals?

- What's a "stretch goal" that will push you forward and force you to grow even if you ultimately fall short?

CHAPTER FOUR:
FINDING AND MAINTAINING MOTIVATION

Outside of God's divine power, motivation might be the most powerful force in the entire world. Motivation has played a role in everything done by humankind throughout the course of history. Every idea, decision, and initiative was born out of motivation. To put it simply, someone decided that they wanted to do something, and the rest was history.

Motivation is also a complicated topic for several reasons. First of all, some people view motivation as cliched, stigmatized, or, for lack of a better word, cheesy. They imagine a motivational speaker yelling at them, [6] or they picture one of their friends on social media who's always posting selfies after their workout or taking pictures of their plant-based lunch. There's nothing wrong with eating this way, but I'll have a Spicy Chicken Sandwich and a Large Chick-fil-A Waffle Potato Fries, please.

---

[6] He probably eats a steady diet of government cheese and lives in a van down by the river (look up "Matt Foley" on YouTube if you don't get this reference).

More importantly, for the sake of our discussion, many people believe that motivation is coincidental and a trait that only certain people possess. You'll hear people say things like, "I'm feeling demotivated right now" or "I can't figure out how to motivate myself." They imagine an alternate reality where they feel a strong sense of motivation to work toward a particular goal or outcome. Not only is this perspective inaccurate, but it's actually quite harmful.

The truth is that motivation is much more an equalizer than it is a differentiator. It may sound like a hot take, but I believe we all have the same amount of motivation. Think about it. Motivation plays a role in everything we do. We tend to associate motivation with tasks that are difficult, but motivation is present in any activity. The outcome doesn't matter.

For example, people often associate motivation with exercise. Imagine you're thinking about waking up early to go to the gym or jogging around your neighborhood. Let's take a look at each of your options and consider what motivations might be coming into play:

- **Going to the gym.** You're motivated to get in better physical shape (lose weight, burn fat, etc.). You may also crave the emotional and mental benefits that come from being physically active.
- **Stay in bed and sleep in.** You're motivated by the physical and mental comfort that comes from maintaining the status quo and avoiding hard tasks.

You can see how whatever decision you make involves motivation. It's also important to point out that we often feel competing motivations. The above scenario is a great example. At the same time, you may desire both outcomes. You want to get your workout in, but you also want to remain comfortable.

Motivation isn't an all-or-nothing game. When you choose to do something, it isn't because your motivation is 100% aligned with that particular task. You simply feel more motivated to pursue one outcome than any other.

This principle is eye-opening for several reasons. First of all, it increases our awareness about how our motivation works when we're making decisions. More importantly, it shows that the gap between where you are right now and improving yourself or making better decisions isn't as big as you thought. You don't have to feel 100% motivated to exercise, eat better, start a business, clean your garage, read your Bible, or call your parents. If you can muster at least 51%, you can get over the hump and begin building momentum.

So, if we only have to get to 51%, why is it so hard to feel motivated to do hard things? Honestly, we have our brains to blame. Our brains are hardwired to prioritize the most certain outcome or results. Usually, this is whatever reward we can experience sooner or whatever reward is based on past experience. In the above example of choosing to get up to exercise or stay in bed, it's easier to stay in bed because the reward (maintaining comfort) can be experienced immediately.

Here's what we must realize: while both options have a potential reward, they also each come with a cost. This is true for every decision that we make. Every action includes both a cost and a reward. Let's take a second look at the above scenario to understand what's going on:

- **Going to the gym.** *Cost:* Discomfort from exerting yourself. Inability to maintain comfort. *Reward:* Better physical condition. Release of endorphins. Improved emotional and psychological state.
- **Stay in bed and sleep in.** *Cost:* Unrealized potential. Failure to improve physical condition. Feeling sluggish and de-energized during the day. *Reward:* Maintain comfort. Avoid doing something challenging and exerting yourself.

Did you notice that going to the gym offered a long-term reward for a short-term cost, while staying in bed produced a short-term reward followed by a long-term cost? This is the issue many of us experience as we try to utilize our motivation. Since we're hardwired for instant gratification, we choose the shiny object in front of us, even if we must pay for it in the long run.

Although we've identified more problems than solutions so far, we're making progress. If you're going to leverage your motivation in a way that helps you accomplish your most important goals, understanding you have as much motivation as anyone else is a great first step. It's pretty empowering when you realize you have the same amount of internal motivation as Martin Luther King, Michael Jordan, Nelson Mandela, Steve Jobs, or Thomas Edison. It's also encouraging to learn that the gap between *having* motivation and *using* motivation isn't as vast as you may have thought before. We're headed in the right direction, but there's still something missing.

While these concepts certainly move the needle, this next idea may be the biggest one of all. Obviously, having motivation isn't all that matters. What separates successful people from those who never recognize their potential isn't the amount of motivation they have but it's their ability to focus or direct their motivation in a way that helps them reach their goals.

Here's the cool thing - you can control your motivation. Perhaps you can't objectively choose the target of your motivation in every situation, but you can impact the direction of your motivation both directly and indirectly. This is the next step in our pursuit of motivation. Once you learn how much motivation actually exists inside of you, the next step is learning about how motivation actually works and how we can align our motivation with our goals.

Common Myths about Motivation

As we consider how to take charge of our motivation, we must continue to examine the limiting beliefs and false narratives we bring to the table. I told you this before, but motivation is often misunderstood. Your perspective on motivation could be holding you back, even if there's no truth or validity behind the way you approach the topic. Let's consider some of the most common myths about motivation.

Myth One: Motivation is constant

When we know somebody who's accomplishing huge goals and constantly doing hard things, it's easy to assume they hit the ground running every morning. The truth is that finding and maintaining motivation usually isn't a linear process. You'll have days where you feel highly motivated to work on your goals, and you'll have days where you feel exhausted or drained.

If you have days where you don't feel motivated to work and be productive, it doesn't mean there's anything wrong with you. It's simply a part of the human experience. Rather than beating yourself up for not feeling energized each day, try to create systems and habits that keep you on track even on days when you don't feel as motivated as you normally do.

Myth Two: Motivation eliminates the need for discipline

Motivation and discipline are related, but they aren't identical to one another. Many of us don't like the word "discipline." We may remember punishments from our parents when we were children. Or we may think about a boring, regimented lifestyle that's never any fun.

This view represents an inaccurate understanding of discipline. It's true that discipline requires some effort, but a disciplined life can be highly fulfilling and enjoyable. Discipline strengthens the impact of your motivation by making it more tangible or actionable.

Imagine that you feel motivated to start a business. You're excited about turning your hobby or passion into a side hustle. This could be a great idea, but how do you put this motivation into action? You'll incorporate disciplines like posting on social media, reaching out to potential customers, and networking with other professionals in your area. Your motivation to start a business manifests itself in small actions that will help you make progress toward reaching your ultimate goal.

Motivation without discipline can be helpful, but ultimately, discipline is the vehicle that gets us where we want to go. Motivation is simply the fuel that drives the discipline.

Myth Three: Motivation guarantees success

This probably won't be news to you, but human beings like control. We appreciate when things are black-and-white. We find comfort in seeing a clear cause-and-effect progression that connects a certain outcome to a particular task. When this happens, we don't have to wonder about what we should expect.

It shouldn't surprise you that life rarely works out this perfectly, and this includes the use of our motivation. Understanding and applying your motivation will increase your chances of success, but it can't guarantee anything. Motivation is only one ingredient in the recipe for success. The list also includes complex factors such as daily habits, resources, timing, connections, and external circumstances.

If you've ever read Stephen Covey's book *The Seven Habits of Highly Effective People*,[7] you're familiar with his teachings on the circle of concern and the circle of influence. The circle of concern includes issues and topics we care about but cannot control. The circle of influence, on the other hand, contains all the areas where we can have an effect or impact. For example, whether or not someone offers you a job, invites you to an event, or responds to your email falls into the circle of concern. On the other hand, the quality of your resume, the manner in which you treat people, and the wording and timing of your request are all within your circle of influence.

What about success? What circle does it fit into? It's hard to say, and it depends partially on how you define success. Generally speaking, success doesn't fully fall into either. We can't fully influence whether or not we experience the success we desire. However, I would argue that motivation (mostly) falls under the circle of influence. We can guide and direct our motivation, which will put us in a better position to achieve greater success.

These aren't the only three myths regarding motivation, but they are among the most common and the most detrimental. Now that we've eliminated these myths from our understanding, let's replace them with some more constructive beliefs and principles.

---

[7]   https://www.amazon.com/Habits-Highly-Effective-People-Anniversary/dp/1511317299

Four Essential Truths About Motivation

Let me clarify that I'm not trying to reduce motivation, a complex field of scientific study, into a few simple statements or concepts. While I hope and pray that you find this information helpful, I know it's impossible to fully understand motivation without taking the neurological and psychological elements of motivation into account.

At the same time, I don't think you need to be a neuroscientist in order to understand how motivation works at a basic level. Now that we've clarified a few common misconceptions, let's look at a few practical ideas that can help you leverage the power of your motivation to its full potential.

Truth One: Motivation and willpower aren't the same thing

Do you remember learning about the difference between speed and velocity in your middle school physics class? If you don't remember, speed is simply the rate at which an object moves, while velocity is speed in a particular direction. While speed and velocity are similar, they aren't terms that can be used interchangeably.

This is a good metaphor to help us understand the difference between motivation and willpower. Motivation is to speed as willpower is to velocity. In other words, willpower is the specific application of motivation to a particular task or outcome. While we all possess the same amount of motivation and utilize motivation in each decision, willpower can wax and wane depending on the individual person and situation. Willpower is a lot like a muscle - the more you use it, the more tired it becomes.

However, you can prime your environment to create situations that require less willpower. Maybe you create accountability in the form of a commitment device, such as signing up for a workout class or telling a friend about a goal you have. Maybe you remove the junk food from your pantry when you're trying to lose weight. These subtle changes will decrease the need for willpower, allowing you to save it for other situations.

Truth Two: Your unconscious mind plays a key role in your motivation

I said above that you don't have to be a neuroscientist in order to understand the general workings of motivation. I also don't feel like you have to have an advanced degree or prior knowledge or experience in order to comprehend the basic science of motivation.

The most important thing you must know about the science of motivation is that your brain produces a chemical called dopamine when it's anticipating the reward. This is surprising because you would probably expect a dopamine release when the reward is experienced, but this isn't actually the case. You may know that there are four steps to building a habit: cue, craving, response, and reward. When a habit begins, the response triggers the reward. However, as your brain begins to sense a predictable pattern, it begins releasing dopamine upon noticing the cue or the craving because it's anticipating your response.

As we come to understand how dopamine works, we can make more informed decisions about the activities we pursue and the situations we put ourselves in. We'll recognize when we're engaging in activities because we want a quick dopamine hit, and we'll be able to remove the cues and cravings so that they don't knock us off course or prevent us from reaching our goals.

Jesus alludes to this concept when He teaches about the sin of adultery in the Sermon on the Mount. His audience would have been familiar with Moses' commandment to avoid adultery. However, Jesus takes it a step further and proclaims that any man who looks at a woman lustfully has already committed adultery in his heart. It's as if Jesus is encouraging us to remove the cue rather than simply trying to avoid the response. He's shifting our attention to the root problem and showing us a more effective approach.

Truth Three: Internal motivators are more powerful than external motivators

Most people are familiar with the two types of motivators. External motivators are things such as money, power, wealth, and success. While these external qualities may seem more attractive at first glance, internal motivators are more powerful and easier to sustain over time. Many of the most popular internal motivators are concepts such as purpose and core values, which we've already talked about in detail in this book.

The key here is understanding what you truly desire. Some activities may seem like they have intrinsic value even though they are only a means to an end. As Dave

Ramsey wrote in his book "EntreLeadership," You can climb the ladder of success only to realize it was leaned against the wrong building the entire time. Furthermore, external motivators like money and prestige are often reflective of deeper desires. You may crave the security that money provides (an internal motivator) more than you actually care about the dollar amount in your bank account.

How to Eat an Elephant

If I could offer you one final piece of advice as you think about how to understand and apply these teachings on motivation, I would encourage you to dream big and think small.

That may sound like an oxymoron, but hear me out. Let's start by clarifying what it means to think big. Craig Groeschel, the Senior Pastor of LifeChurch and the host of the Craig Groeschel Leadership Podcast, often says that people tend to overestimate what's possible in the short term while underestimating what they can do in the long term. You may be overly bullish about what you can do in a few weeks, but what could you do in the next five years if you made a decision and a commitment today? With your purpose and values in mind, let me challenge you to begin thinking about your next big dream or goal.

At the same time, you'll have an easier time exercising your motivation if your goal seems attainable. You've probably heard the popular adage about the best way to eat an elephant ("one bite at a time.") Rome wasn't built in a day, but you'll be amazed at what you can accomplish through daily discipline and consistent effort. Take your long-term goal and break it down into smaller steps, and you'll soon find that finding and maintaining motivation is much easier than it was before.

We also must remember that Rome wasn't built by one person. You don't have to do everything by yourself. Throw a party and invite your friends over to help you eat the elephant. Not only will this approach be more effective, but it will also be more enjoyable. Life is more fun when you do it with people you love, and goals are the same way. Plus, you won't get sick from trying to eat an entire elephant by yourself.

Alright, enough about eating elephants. I don't want to ruin your next trip to the zoo. What I want you to see as we wrap up this conversation is that motivation has the potential to open big doors and create new and exciting possibilities. At the same time, it's more sustainable to exercise motivation in small quantities. If we really believe that life is a gradual, never-ending pursuit, this is great news. We're running a marathon, not a sprint.

Application Questions

1. If you felt like you had full control over your motivation, what would you do differently?
2. What false narrative or limiting belief about motivation is most prevalent in your life? How is it holding you back?
3. How will you adjust your motivation to pursue your goals and live the life that you truly desire?

CHAPTER FIVE:
CULTIVATING CHARACTER

I love the idea of having a garden. I dream about growing fresh tomatoes, cilantro, and onions and making delicious homemade salsa. I've tried several times to start one, but it never works out.

To tell you the truth, I strongly dislike pulling weeds. Even when I decide to give gardening another try and promise myself that things will be different, weeds always take over, and my dream of homemade salsa goes by the wayside. As much as I enjoy the Jalapeno Salsa that comes with my Chick-fil-A Hash Brown Scramble Burrito with Nuggets, I didn't do the work to create it myself.

Multiple failed attempts have taught me how much work it takes to keep a garden. A garden doesn't happen by accident, and the quality of your garden is a reflection of the work you're willing to put in. Your labor will be fruitful if you're willing to put in the necessary amount of time and energy. On the other hand, if you don't plan and prepare properly, you won't get the results you want.

I believe that what's true about gardening is also true about your character. Strong character doesn't happen accidentally. If you want your character to grow and develop to the point where it produces a positive result in your life, it's going to take time and focused attention.

First, you'll need to create an environment where good character can grow and flourish. Think of this as your garden. Once your garden is ready to go, you'll have to choose what seeds to plant and determine how to best care for them so that they take root and produce fruit. You'll need to be willing to identify and pull weeds so that they don't choke out your crops and destroy your garden.

This may sound like a lot of work, and it is. However, like everything else in The Never-Ending Pursuit, it's not a race. You'll spend the rest of your life working on developing your character, and the journey is just as valuable as the destination. More importantly, doing the hard work of cultivating character will help you grow in your ability to pursue your purpose, embody your values, and achieve your long-term goals.

In the rest of this chapter, we'll walk through each of these steps in detail. You'll learn how to prime your environment for ongoing character development, and you'll have a clear sense of what this process will require of you.

Building Your Garden

Jesus often used farming examples and illustrations in His parables since they would have been easy for His listeners to understand. In one particular example, Jesus sets the scene by describing a farmer who was scattering seeds across different surfaces. It doesn't take long for us to see how much it matters where the seed lands:

> *"Listen! A farmer went out to plant some seeds. As he scattered them across his field, some seeds fell on a footpath, and the birds came and ate them. Other seeds fell on shallow soil with underlying rock. The seeds sprouted quickly because the soil was shallow. But the plants soon wilted under the hot sun, and since they didn't have deep roots, they died. Other seeds fell among thorns that grew up and choked out the tender plants. Still other seeds fell on fertile soil, and they produced a crop that was thirty, sixty, and even a hundred times as much as had been planted! Anyone with ears to hear should listen and understand."*

> Matthew 13:3-9, NLT

Soon after, Jesus explained the meaning behind this metaphor to His disciples:

> *" 'Now listen to the explanation of the parable about the farmer planting seeds: The seed that fell on the footpath represents those who hear the message about the Kingdom and don't understand it. Then the evil one comes and snatches away the seed that was planted in their hearts. The seed on the rocky soil represents those who hear the message and immediately receive it with joy. But since they don't have deep roots, they don't last long. They fall away as soon as they have problems or are persecuted for believing God's word. The seed that fell among the thorns*

represents those who hear God's word, but all too quickly the message is crowded out by the worries of this life and the lure of wealth, so no fruit is produced. The seed that fell on good soil represents those who truly hear and understand God's word and produce a harvest of thirty, sixty, or even a hundred times as much as had been planted!' "

Matthew 13:18-23 NLT

Jesus' message is clear. Ultimately, it doesn't matter what seeds you're planting if the soil isn't ready to receive the seeds and help them grow. Before you can begin strengthening your character, you must develop a suitable environment where your character can thrive.

In many ways, this begins with your attitude and your expectations. In his book "Do Over," Jon Acuff writes that we can all choose our attitude and adjust our expectations regardless of the situations we find ourselves in. Remember what Chuck Swindoll once said, "Life is 10% what happens to you and 90% how you react." You may not have full control over every situation, but you can choose how you interpret and interact with your surroundings.

We should also reject a fixed mindset and adopt a growth mindset instead. Someone who has a fixed mindset is unwilling to acknowledge areas for potential growth and improvement. They lack the humility to recognize that they haven't yet reached their potential. On the other hand, a person who has a growth mindset is willing to accept feedback and understand that they are still a work in progress. If you share constructive feedback with somebody who has a fixed mindset, they may deflect, blame, or say, "That's just the way I am." If you give the same feedback to somebody with a growth mindset, they will accept responsibility and promise to work on improving. As we read in Proverbs 9:8 (NLT), "So don't bother correcting mockers; they will only hate you. But correct the wise, and they will love you."

If I could offer one more piece of advice, I would encourage you to think about the value of character development. If you were a person of character, how would that impact your individual pursuit? What would that do for the people around you? What difference would it make for your career, your family, your church, and your community? If you can define the outcome or impact you're working toward, you'll have an easier time pushing yourself and maintaining long-term motivation, even when things become difficult.

If you learn how to choose your attitude, adjust your expectations, and adopt a growth mindset, you're well on your way to creating a situation ripe for character development. Envisioning the value that your character development can provide to yourself and to those around you will act as the fertilizer that complements good soil and facilitates growth. Now that you've set up your metaphorical garden, you can start thinking about what character seeds you'll plant.

Choosing Your Plants

Typically, gardeners will choose plants based on the type of fruits or vegetables they want to produce. If I'm craving salsa, I'll plant vegetables like tomatoes and cilantro. If I'd rather have a fresh fruit salad, I may try planting raspberries or strawberries. Regardless, there's some degree of initial planning or forethought required. You don't simply plant the first thing that comes to mind or the first thing you come across.

Attempting to build character requires getting clear about what you hope to accomplish. Simply targeting character growth isn't necessarily wrong, but it's also a little too ambiguous to have a significant outcome. You're better off clarifying where you need to grow and what you hope to accomplish.

So, what can (or should) that targeted growth be for you? It depends on several factors. Part of the decision is based on what you value. Another part has to do with your current weaknesses or limitations. Your situation also plays an important role. In short, what do you care about, where are you right now, and what's missing from your life?

There are some qualities that have universal value for all people. I can't help but think about the Fruits of the Spirit laid out by Paul in Galatians 5: "But the Holy Spirit produces this kind of fruit in our lives: love, joy, peace, patience, kindness, goodness, faithfulness, gentleness, and self-control. There is no law against these things!" (Galatians 5:22-23, NLT)

Obviously, you can't go wrong working to grow in any of these areas. However, it can be hard to work on nine goals at the same time. You may have more success if you choose two or three specific traits to work on at a time. If patience doesn't come naturally to you, working on patience could be a great place to start. If you find yourself becoming overly cynical or pessimistic, look for opportunities to cultivate joy in your life.

This type of focused attention will require a few sacrifices from you. First of all, you'll need to be willing to become uncomfortable. As human beings, we're hardwired to pursue and maintain comfort at all costs. However, there's no such thing as growth without struggle. It's the reason why your muscles get sore during a workout, and it's the same reason why you often feel closer to another person after enduring a trial or a difficult season together.

It probably also isn't something you can do with your own power. This is where the Holy Spirit comes into play. There's something beautiful that happens when you submit to God's power when you're attempting to change your heart or your mindset. Your faith will grow as you submit to God's power and trust that God will do for you what you aren't able to do for yourself.

Finally, this takes vulnerability. There's a growing stigma that exists when we talk about vulnerability. Vulnerability doesn't require you emptying all of your baggage onto a table for everyone to see, and it doesn't always come with tears or major confessions. However, there's always an expression of weakness, to some degree, when vulnerability is expressed. We must be willing to show up as we actually are, both for ourselves and for others, if we're going to grow in character.

Planting the seeds of stronger character is certainly a process. Once the seeds are in the ground, you'll need to nurture them and give them time to fully grow and develop. However, if you're willing to commit to consistency and intentionality, you'll slowly begin to notice a change in yourself. You'll also need to be prepared to deal with obstacles along the way in the form of weeds.

Pulling Weeds

Just like every garden grows weeds, everyone will deal with temptation or distractions at times. It's not representative of any outstanding character flaws you may still have. It's simply how life works. Knowing that weeds will grow is important, and so is understanding the responsibility we have to deal with weeds as they come up.

Immediately after sharing the Parable of the Sower (which we referenced above), Jesus tells another story about a farmer:

> Here is another story Jesus told: "The Kingdom of Heaven is like a farmer who planted good seed in his field. But that night as the workers slept, his enemy came and planted weeds among the wheat, then slipped away. When the crop began to grow and produce grain, the weeds also grew. "The farmer's workers went to him and said, 'Sir, the field where you planted that good seed is full of

weeds! Where did they come from?' "'An enemy has done this!' the farmer exclaimed. "'Should we pull out the weeds?' they asked. "'No,' he replied, 'you'll uproot the wheat if you do. Let both grow together until the harvest. Then I will tell the harvesters to sort out the weeds, tie them into bundles, and burn them, and to put the wheat in the barn.'"

Matthew 13:24-30, NLT

There's an eschatological element in this story that speaks to the question people often ask about the presence of evil in the world. In short, many wonder how a good God could allow evil to exist in the world because of the heartbreak and struggle evil creates. Our assumption is that the world would somehow be better if evil didn't exist. While I do believe that it would ultimately be better, we must also remember (as Paul tells us in 1 Corinthians) that God's ways are far better and wiser than our ways.

This story reflects this truth. The farmer teaches his workers that something about the presence of weeds enhances the quality or strength of the grain as it grows. The weeds shouldn't remain in the garden forever, the farmer says. However, they also shouldn't be immediately removed.

What a perfect metaphor for us to consider as we continue thinking about the metaphor of a lifelong, Never-Ending Pursuit of personal growth and development. This story reminds us that we'll never stop facing trials, distractions, temptations, and setbacks.

While this won't be pleasant or enjoyable, there's something about the presence of these difficulties that's actually for our benefit.

Jesus isn't unaware of what this experience is like. As the writer of Hebrews tells us, Jesus was tempted in the same ways as we are, yet He did not sin (Hebrews 4:15). Jesus experienced the worst that the world could throw at Him as He faced physical torment and emotional ridicule on the cross. He persevered through all this and provided us with an example of what it looks like to stay strong in the midst of tribulation.

If Jesus has to deal with weeds, so will we. It's important to recognize that we can't eliminate every weed in our garden. As long as we live in an imperfect world, there will be weeds. However, there's a difference between accepting that we can't deal with every single weed and ignoring their existence entirely. We must remain aware of the weeds – and the impact they have on our character development – at all times.

As we become aware of what weeds exist in our garden, we'll learn how to address them. Some weeds are easy to pull. There's no reason to stay in a bad relationship or knowingly put yourself in a harmful situation. When we spot these weeds, we must call them out and address them immediately.

Over time, you'll identify weeds that are more difficult to uproot. Perhaps you relate to Paul when he speaks about the "thorn in his side" in 2 Corinthians 12. When this happens, you'll stay mindful of their presence, and we will look for opportunities to grow and stretch even in the midst of hardship. Trust in God's power to help you overcome, and remember that His power is made perfect in human weakness.

Your Character Building Plan

For some people, building and maintaining a garden may seem like a primarily passive activity. Obviously, you'll have to do the work of laying soil, planting seeds, and (unfortunately) pulling weeds. At the same time, once the seed is in the ground, there doesn't seem to be much you can do besides performing occasional maintenance and waiting for the plant to sprout.

This perspective isn't fully accurate. A garden requires constant care and attention in order to grow strong and healthy plants. I've realized this many times in the past as I increasingly grow impatient waiting for my vegetables to sprout, only to realize that weeds have taken over.

The hard work isn't over once your plants are in the ground, and the same is true for character development. It's not a passive activity. It requires constant focus and energy. You'll be tempted to drift back into old habits. Choosing what's easy or comfortable will always be appealing.

If you're going to see powerful transformation or long-term results, you'll have to commit to constant focus and ongoing action. Choosing the right structure or process is important, but once you've identified what you plan to do, the work is far from over. Now it's time for execution. It will be grueling at times, and you may want to quit.

However, you constantly make the choice to continue because you know what you're seeking to accomplish. It's not easy, but you knew going in that it wouldn't be. You continue to move forward not because it's comfortable or convenient but because you know there's value in both the journey and the destination.

I'll leave you with the words of James from James 5:7-8 (NLT): "Dear brothers and sisters, be patient as you wait for the Lord's return. Consider the farmers who patiently wait for the rains in the fall and in the spring. They eagerly look for the valuable harvest to ripen. You, too, must be patient. Take courage, for the coming of the Lord is near." The harvest is coming, and we'll continue to cultivate our gardens as we wait on God's perfect timing.

Application questions

1. What practical steps can you take to "build your garden" or cultivate an environment that will facilitate the ongoing development of strong character?
2. What character seeds will you plant in your garden first?
3. Are you aware of any weeds that currently exist in your garden? How will you address them?

Chapter Six:
Pursuing Integrity

I've always been intrigued by the Sermon on the Mount. And why shouldn't I be? It's essentially the most famous sermon ever given by the greatest person to walk the Earth.

One of the repeating themes in the Sermon on the Mount that stands out to me is the concept of receiving a reward. On three different occasions, Jesus calls the Pharisees out for their public acts of righteousness and tells them they have already received their full reward.

I find this interesting because it reminds me that you can do the right thing for the wrong reason. There's nothing wrong with the behaviors Jesus is talking about. I think we would all agree that praying, fasting, and giving to the needy are positive actions. The issue isn't what the Pharisees are doing. It's the motives behind the actions that are the problem.

I think this is an important principle to consider as we finish our conversation on character and move into a discussion about integrity. When you do the right thing for the wrong reasons, you do a disservice to yourself and to others. You diminish the impact of your activity, and any positive contribution you make comes without any sort of relational or self-sacrificial element.

For the pursuit of character to have a substantial or lasting effect, it must be driven by integrity. In other words, your character stands on the foundation of your integrity. Character determines what you do, and integrity influences why you do what you do. Let's dig deeper into integrity to fully understand the critical role it plays.

What is integrity?

Webster's dictionary defines integrity as a firm adherence to a code of especially moral or artistic values. It compares the concept of integrity to the quality of being incorruptible, meaning incapable of being swayed or bribed. To me, integrity is doing what's right regardless of the cost or outcome. Living from integrity requires holding true to your values and convictions, even in the face of opposition.

The story of the Good Samaritan in the Gospel of Luke is one of the most well-known passages in the entire Bible. It's also one of the best narratives in Scripture to consider as we work to develop our understanding of integrity.

The scene begins in Luke 10:25, but it's important to remember that immediately before this story, Jesus is celebrating the ironic reversal of wisdom and knowledge against society's expectations. He looks to heaven and praises God for hiding wisdom from so-called wise men and choosing to share important things with "the childlike" instead (Luke 10:21, NLT). Biblical authors often place stories next to each other to make a point, and as we dive into this narrative, we'll quickly see why this proximity is important.

Sometime after Jesus made this declaration, an expert in the law brought Jesus a question. "What must I do to inherit eternal life?" While the question seems innocent enough at first glance, we know from Luke's commentary that the question was posed in an attempt to test Jesus (and, potentially, accuse him of blasphemy or heresy against traditional Jewish teachings based on what He said).

Jesus responds with a question, as He often would, and asks the man how he interprets the Law of Moses. The man quotes two key passages from the Torah (Deuteronomy 6:5 and Leviticus 19:18), which emphasize the importance of loving God and loving others. Jesus affirms the man's response and promises that he will live if he does such things.

However, the man has an agenda, so the conversation doesn't end there. He knows the command to love his neighbor as his own self, but he wants to know who his neighbor is. Like his first query, this question would seem fairly innocent if we didn't understand the man's intentions, which are made clear in Luke's commentary. This man doesn't appear interested in expanding his definition of the people he would consider to be his "neighbor." He wants to hear Jesus say who it's acceptable to leave out.

While it's easy to pile on this man at this point for being blatantly exclusive, it's worth pointing out that this wasn't an individual concern. His feelings didn't only reflect his own views. Instead, his prejudice was reflective of the Jewish people group as a whole.

Jews had strong rivalries and feuds with certain groups of people dating back hundreds of years. The thought of associating with people such as Samaritans was outrageous. Both sides felt strong animosity towards the other, mainly centered around disagreements regarding the Temple and the Torah. Jews considered Samaritans to be ritually unclean and refused to eat or intermarry with them.

If you've heard the story of the Good Samaritan before, you're beginning to understand the shock factor on a deeper level:

> *"Jesus replied with a story: 'A Jewish man was traveling from Jerusalem down to Jericho, and he was attacked by bandits. They stripped him of his clothes, beat him up, and left him half dead beside the road.*
>
> *By chance a priest came along. But when he saw the man lying there, he crossed to the other side of the road and passed him by. A Temple assistant walked over and looked at him lying there, but he also passed by on the other side.*
>
> *Then a despised Samaritan came along, and when he saw the man, he felt compassion for him. Going over to him, the Samaritan soothed his wounds with olive oil and wine and bandaged them. Then*

he put the man on his own donkey and took him to an inn, where he took care of him. The next day he handed the innkeeper two silver coins, telling him, 'Take care of this man. If his bill runs higher than this, I'll pay you the next time I'm here.'

'Now which of these three would you say was a neighbor to the man who was attacked by bandits?' Jesus asked.

The man replied, 'The one who showed him mercy.'

Then Jesus said, 'Yes, now go and do the same.'"

Luke 10:30-37, NLT

Despite the past tension and the perception among Jews that Samaritans were inherently evil or unclean, Jesus presents the Samaritan as the hero in this story. This man also does an excellent job of portraying our working definition of integrity, whether he recognized it or not, by choosing to do the right thing regardless of the cost or the outcome. Upon seeing the man, he feels compassion for him. It's impossible to know if this is instantaneous compassion or if the man had been working to develop compassion through his character-building efforts.

Regardless, compassion shows up in the form of a feeling that leads to action. He approaches the man, treats his wounds, and puts him on his donkey to bring him to a local hotel. When they arrive, he gives the innkeeper two silver coins, an amount equal to two days' wages, and promises to pay the difference when he comes back if more money is necessary to treat him. Again, we don't know if the man passed by the inn regularly or if he was going to make a special return trip because of this arrangement. Either way, his attention to the Jewish man didn't end after he checked into the inn. He was still choosing to participate in the man's ongoing care.

By taking this approach, the Samaritan is prioritizing the Jewish man's needs, regardless of what it demands from him. He doesn't care about the cost of the hotel. He doesn't care about the lost time or the detour on his journey. He seemingly doesn't care about the perception he may receive from others. Although there weren't glaring physical differences (such as skin color or traditional dress) between Jews and Samaritans, it's possible that someone would have seen the Samaritan attending to the Jewish man on the road or carrying him on his donkey. Even if that were the case, it didn't impact the Samaritan's attitude or actions.

As we consider the implications of this story and the Samaritan man's practical display of integrity and compassion, I wonder what would be possible if we took a similar approach. What if we became hyper-concerned with doing what's right, even when the cost was high and the outcome was uncertain? What if we disregarded societal expectations of who was deserving of love and compassion and made caring for the hurting and the marginalized our primary focus?

This is what lived integrity looks like. The costs can be steep. If nothing else, we're disrupting the status quo, and it can be uncomfortable. Most people prefer to avoid rocking the boat at all costs. Acting from integrity often means we have to be willing to speak up when something isn't right or when it's harming other people.

At the same time, the outcome is uncertain. The end goal isn't always clear. Our actions may not produce the results that we desire, but that's ultimately not what's most important. What matters is that we are living from our values and emphasizing the greater good.

It's also worth pointing out that the pursuit of integrity will do something profound inside of you. The application of integrity to difficult situations and the pursuit of integrity in situations that could adversely affect your life will challenge you. However, in that challenge, you'll find numerous opportunities for character-building and personal development. You'll become the type of person who doesn't react to momentary desires or temporary pressure. Instead, your primary goal will be to exercise your convictions and do what's right or good.

Prioritizing Integrity

You now have a clearer picture of the relationship between character and integrity, and you understand how integrity must take precedence. So, how does this look, practically speaking? What principles or disciplines can you embody to make this concept real in your everyday life?

First things first, you must accept what you can and can't control. Both perspectives are important, and you may find one is harder for you to adopt. Some people struggle with reconciling what they can't control. I find it's especially difficult for people with a Type-A, go-getter personality. They sometimes feel frustrated that other people don't act in the same way or move at the same pace. If this describes you, focus on bringing your best to the domains that are within your power and trust that others are doing the best they can, even when it doesn't appear to be the case.

Others live in ignorance of the amount of agency they actually have. They choose to focus on what they can't control, and they refuse to accept responsibility to choose a different course or direction in life. While there are certainly some things we can't control, each person has some degree of influence. If nothing else, you are fully capable of leading yourself, and that alone is a tremendous opportunity.

You may be wondering what does this have to do with integrity. Being able to reconcile what you can and can't control will enable you to detach yourself from results (which you can't fully control) and focus instead on your own actions. In short, you're trusting the process, which incorporates not only what you do but the reason why you do what you do. You have faith that if you act with integrity, the results and outcomes will sort themselves out.

Is there a chance that things won't work out? Of course. Life isn't fair, especially when the right actions have negative consequences while the wrong decisions are rewarded. At the same time, if you act with integrity and experience negative consequences, you'll be able to live with yourself because you're at peace with the reasons behind your actions. When you live with this perspective on integrity and value the application and practice of integrity in all situations, your definition of success begins to shift in a new direction.

A New Picture of Success

How would you define success? It's an intentionally broad question. I would imagine that if you asked a room of 100 people to write down their ideal vision of success, you would get a wide range of answers. Many people think of success in terms of external factors like money, power, and prestige. You can find temporary satisfaction in each of these areas, but it's short-lived.

As you progress further in your Never-Ending Pursuit, success begins to look different. You become more introspective, and you value internal, personal qualities more than material goods or misleading measures of external success. You realize that your value comes not from what you have or what you accomplish but from who you are as a person.

That's the thing about living with integrity. As you grow to appreciate the value of living with integrity at all times, regardless of the outcome, the exercise of integrity becomes the true measure of success. In other words, the process matters more to you than the result. You don't care as much about where you arrive because you find such great value and fulfillment in the journey.

It's the person who's willing to speak up for what's right and wrong, not because they are thinking about how others perceive them, but because they care about fighting against injustice. It's the man who stays faithful to his wife through several decades of marriage, not because he's afraid of the consequences of infidelity, but because he loves and honors his wife. It's the pastor who spends long hours visiting shut-ins, not because it's listed in his job description but because he wants to be an encouragement to those who feel lonely and isolated.

The reward in each of these examples is hard to fully grasp or understand, but that's not the point. Integrity isn't about doing the right thing because you desire some sort of reward. It's about doing the right thing simply because it's the right thing. Over time, the pursuit itself becomes the ultimate source of fulfillment. Your goal isn't to win the game, so to speak. Your goal is to keep playing the game.

I think this is the kind of life that Jesus wants us to live. Galatians 6:9-10 (NLT) says, "So let's not get tired of doing what is good. At just the right time, we will reap a harvest of blessings if we don't give up. Therefore, whenever we have the opportunity, we should do good to everyone— especially to those in the family of faith." Whether that harvest is for our benefit or for someone else's is impossible to say, and ultimately, it doesn't matter because God is always faithful to His promises. We're just here to do the right things, and we know that has inherent value even if it doesn't immediately present itself.

As you begin to adopt true character and integrity, you position yourself as the type of person who can rally others to work for the greater good. Leading and influencing others should not be about personal gain but about pursuing a vision that impacts your entire team, organization, or community in a positive way. The importance of strong leadership can't be undervalued, which is why it's the next move we're going to make.

Application questions

1. In your own words, describe the intersection between character and integrity. What does it look like for you to live out both qualities in your life?

2. How does the story of Jesus and Zacchaeus shape your definition of integrity?

3. Think about a situation in your life where acting with integrity could lead to conflict or discomfort. How committed are you to taking this step?

CHAPTER SEVEN:
DEVELOPING LEADERSHIP SKILLS

What is a leader?

This is a big question, and you could answer it in many different ways. Some people will picture a leader as the loudest voice in the room. Others will think of a leader as the face of a company or organization, the one who receives praise and accolades when things go well (and criticism when times aren't as good).

No matter what picture comes to mind when you think about a leader, you likely have a preconceived notion of what a leader typically looks like or what it means to be a leader. You may not feel like you're a natural-born leader, and you may question what value this chapter has for you.

Let me encourage you not to skip this chapter or assume that this message doesn't apply to you. Sure, there's a chance that you never have direct reports at work. You might never be in a position where you're making hard decisions on behalf of the group or standing at the front of the pack and encouraging those who are behind you to keep moving in the direction that you set. However, we're all called to be a leader in some form or fashion.

The simplest definition of leader that I have ever heard comes from Webster's Dictionary: "A leader is a person who leads." We're all called to take on this responsibility, even if we don't recognize it initially. For starters, each person must learn to lead himself or herself. This is a task that doesn't receive as much credit or respect as it deserves. You are primarily responsible for choosing your attitude, your perspective on life, and the way that you interpret and respond to situations both inside and outside of your control.

This is one of the most important applications of leadership, and it's one we need to spend some time talking about in order to fully understand why it matters - especially if you get caught in an unexpected monsoon while on a family vacation.

How to Lead Yourself

You never picture your beach day ending with your family being escorted off the premises by a lifeguard, but that's exactly what happened to the Grimms during a recent vacation.

Just to clarify, we didn't do anything dangerous or disruptive. There was simply a massive lightning storm that erupted shortly after we set up for the day. After we were asked to leave the beach, we hid under a nearby shelter, hoping for a quick reprieve. As time went on, we realized our plans for the day were a wash (no pun intended).

Still, I thought I could capitalize on a short break in the storm by running back to our condo with our gear. This ended up being a poor choice. I made it about halfway back relatively dry but was quickly met with a torrential downpour.

My timing was terrible. I thought I made the right move, but at the end of the day, I couldn't control the weather.

I could have gotten mad, but I chose to laugh it off instead. *I would have gotten wet either way after taking a dip in the ocean,* I thought to myself. I still had a refreshing moment, just not the one I expected.

Leading yourself begins by recognizing the amount of autonomy or agency you have over your life. In Chapter Four, as we were talking about motivation, we took a look at Stephen Covey's teachings on the circle of concern and the circle of influence. As a reminder, anything you don't ultimately control fits into the circle of concern. This includes issues like whether or not you get offered your dream job, if someone you're interested in agrees to go on a date with you, or whether or not it rains the day you're planning to hit the beach. Can you be concerned about these things? Sure. Can you force them to go your way? No.

On the other hand, the circle of influence includes all the domains you control yourself. Choosing to spend daily time in Scripture and prayer sits inside your circle of influence. So does planning your day in advance so that you know what you want (or need) to accomplish during your working hours. There's a lot you can't control, but there are still several important choices that you can make for yourself each day.

If you're going to find the most value in your lifelong, Never-Ending Pursuit, and if you're going to transform over time into a person who produces a positive impact and reaches their ultimate potential, it's absolutely critical that you learn how to lead yourself. You can't wait for others to make key decisions for you. Accountability can be helpful, but you must have some degree of agency in order to take the right steps and build positive habits that keep you on a path toward success and growth.

As I think about self-leadership, I can't help but think about Daniel from the Old Testament. Although the book of Daniel is only twelve chapters long, we learn quite a bit about Daniel's life in a short time. For starters, Daniel chooses not to eat the royal food and wine and chooses to limit himself to water and vegetables (Daniel 1:12). After ten days, Daniel and several of his fellow Israelites appeared much healthier and better nourished than the Babylonians who were eating from the king's table (Daniel 1:15-16). Later in Daniel's life, we learn that he prays three times daily, and he continues to practice this habit despite an edict from King Darius prohibiting the people from praying to anyone besides himself (Daniel 6:10-11).

Despite outside opposition, Daniel displays a strong commitment to leading himself. His actions are committed to his sense of purpose in life (another concept we discussed earlier in this book) and his commitment to honoring God and pursuing righteousness.

The way Daniel carries himself also reflects his level of self-discipline, which is the ability and willingness to sacrifice short-term comfort for long-term growth. Self-discipline and self-leadership walk hand-in-hand with each other. Ultimately, both qualities enhance your ability to practice and implement the principles we read about in God's word.

From Daniel's example, we're reminded of the importance of making daily decisions that contribute to our long-term growth and development. When we make these choices, we're putting ourselves in a position to positively influence others in addition to ourselves. Because of Daniel's commitment to discipline and his determination to do the right thing each time, he was promoted to oversee the whole kingdom alongside each successive ruler. Because he proved he was worthy of trust, he was elevated to key positions of leadership.

Leading Yourself and Others

Like Daniel, if you do a good job of leading yourself, there's a good chance you're put in a place where you're asked to lead others as well. While this can be an unfamiliar and challenging endeavor, it's also a great opportunity to expand your impact and pour into others in a way that benefits your own Never-Ending Pursuit in addition to theirs.

Remember the words of Jesus in Luke 16:10 (NLT): "If you are faithful in little things, you will be faithful in large ones. But if you are dishonest in little things, you won't be honest with greater responsibilities." Your approach won't be consistently different just because the lights get brighter or the stakes get higher. Over time, you'll default back to your standard operating level. If you don't do the hard work of leading yourself, things won't change simply because you're now in a position of authority. On the other hand, if you lead yourself well even when nobody is watching, you'll put yourself in a prime position to shine when it's time to step up to the plate and lead others.

This transition can be challenging because leading others requires a different skill set than leading yourself. If you boil leadership down to its most basic essence, leadership is influencing an outcome that may not have happened otherwise. Leaders are typically innovative, creative, and driven to achieve results.

When you're leading yourself, you're the only person you have to convince, and you're generally agreeable with yourself. Sure, you may struggle to decide what to watch on TV or what to eat for dinner, but those internal debates are usually short-lived and relatively civil. You don't have to convince anyone else to take your side or see the world the way you do.

This all changes when it's time to lead others. All of a sudden, direction isn't the only important factor. Because you have to make sure everyone else is on board with the path you're walking and the outcome you're pursuing, pace also becomes important. The best leaders aren't walking fifty feet in front of the group they are guiding. They identify the destination, but they also walk in pace with their team.

When I was 19 years old, I was hiking with a group to the top of Pike's Peak. We were only around 1,000 feet away from the summit when one of my fellow interns told us he couldn't take another step. I so badly wanted to stay with my group and let his group figure out on their own what they would do. Soon after, I realized his group had already gone ahead of him.

I wasn't an expert hiker myself, but I knew I couldn't just leave him behind. Even though I wanted to ignore him, something stirred inside of me that told me I needed to take action. I walked over to him, handed him a packet of jelly left over from my PB&J, and told him to eat this as we took a few small steps at a time. He didn't want to keep going, but I told him we were too close to the top to quit now.

I didn't know this guy well. I had only seen him on campus a few times. However, I couldn't shake the feeling that he was my responsibility at the moment. Perhaps it wasn't my problem based on worldly standards, but I couldn't pass the opportunity to offer him some encouragement and assistance.

When my new friend saw the finish line, tears filled his eyes. He immediately felt empowered to run to the summit, and I followed close behind. At the top of the mountain, he began jumping up and down. "I've never done anything like this in my life! I never thought I could do this!" We hugged and celebrated together as others also high-fived and congratulated him.

I didn't get any "atta-boys" or pats on the back for helping him to the top, but I got something better. My own experience became much more rewarding. I was able to witness someone do something they thought was impossible before. Something amazing took place that day, and I'll forever be grateful for the small part I played.

This story comes to mind whenever I think about leadership. A leader doesn't just show the group how to reach the summit of the mountain, but they empower each person with the strength and the skills they need to get there. Sometimes, that means you move at a slower pace than you would like in order to keep others moving with you.

I believe all leadership starts with self-leadership because you can't lead anybody if you can't lead yourself. More importantly, you won't become a leader worth following if you don't know how to lead yourself. Some people assume that all it takes to be a leader is a position of authority, but this is an incredibly limited and narrow-minded picture of who a true leader is. You shouldn't assume that people will listen to what you have to say or follow the direction you set just because you're in a position of authority. Trust and respect are earned over time, and both can be lost in an instant.

As we make the shift from leading ourselves to leading others, we must consider what it's like to become a leader worth following. We must be self-aware enough to understand what we bring to the table as well as where we can still grow and improve. We must remember that our leadership means nothing if people aren't willing to be led by us.

Ultimately, there are a few key principles worth discussing that will help you develop into a strong, authentic, Christ-centered leader. Let's dig into a few of these qualities below.

Leaders are brave

Anyone with experience in leadership understands that leading others isn't always comfortable. In fact, if you're leading well, you'll frequently find yourself in situations where you can't move forward without intense amounts of courage. Leaders must regularly step outside of their comfort zone, take risks, and galvanize others to move forward, even when facing adversity and uncertainty.

What makes this challenging is that leaders often carry their own fears, insecurities, and uncertainties along with them as they lead. It's easy to fall into the trap of thinking that leaders have it all figured out. Leaders are on a path of growth, struggle, and development like anyone else. They must recognize when this is happening rather than portraying the misconception that they are already a finished product. Nobody is.

Throughout Scripture, we see examples of courageous leaders acting from conviction rather than a desire for comfort or convenience. Think about Esther's decision to go before King Xerxes to tell him about the injustice happening to the Hebrew people in the book of Esther. Another great example comes from Daniel 3 when Shadrach, Meshach, and Abednego boldly choose not to bow before the idol created by King Nebuchadnezzar, even with full awareness of the potential consequences of their actions. Even Gideon, who we discussed back in Chapter One when we were talking about purpose, displayed extreme bravery and assertiveness when he later pursued the massive Midianite army with only 300 men. Gideon's story is especially ironic because he was very timid and cowardly when we first met him.

The common denominator throughout each of these stories (and characters) is an awareness of God's mighty power. Sometimes, acting with courage is only possible when our strength comes from an outside source. Life will wear us down and try to make us focus on things outside of our control. We can fear the unknown, or we can put our trust in the One who created the world and everything in it.

When we find our strength in our faith, we become empowered to live (and lead) through courage regardless of the situations we experience. We also come to appreciate these difficult seasons in a greater way because we recognize the incredible opportunity for growth and development they can provide.

When I was fourteen years old, I went on a mission trip with my youth group to Manhattan. While on the trip, we went to Central Park around midnight to do street ministry. Our leaders broke us up into several groups and sent us out into the park. I found myself paired with a gorgeous girl a few years older than me and another teenage boy who had some intellectual disabilities.

I was terrified. Honestly, putting the three of us in a group together probably wasn't our youth leaders' best idea. There were some great experiences: for example, we met a man named Eddie in the park who was fresh off of a fight with his newlywed wife. We prayed with him and encouraged him. At the same time, we narrowly avoided a potentially dangerous situation.

Toward the end of the night, we were headed back to meet with our leaders and the rest of the group. On the way there, we were surrounded by a group of men dressed in all black. I heard a voice say, "We want to talk to your girl."

I didn't have any time to think about how to respond, but I'm grateful that God gave me the courage I needed to take charge and protect my group. I motioned to the girl and the other boy as if to say, "Don't talk with them. Just keep moving." We put our heads down and continued walking right through the middle of the circle. Thankfully, they didn't follow us.

I would not want to go back and relive that experience. I also wouldn't recommend having a 14-year-old boy lead a group through Central Park at midnight. However, I'm thankful for the lessons I learned that night. If you aspire to be a leader, God's likely going to put you in situations that demand courage and bravery you don't yet have. Next time you find yourself in a challenging situation that demands leading with courage, consider how faith could enable you to move forward in confidence. Remember that your goal isn't to be perfect but to act from your values and convictions while helping others grow and reach their potential.

Leaders aren't afraid of change

Generally, people don't appreciate change. There may be exceptions to the rule, such as receiving a promotion at work or moving into a nicer house. At the same time, these are either changes we seek out or changes that have a clear, tangible, and obvious benefit for us.

Typically, leaders are in charge of initiating change that challenges people at first. They may have a habitual way of doing things, or they may have an attachment to a certain progress or activity because it includes such a high degree of familiarity. These are the people who say, "If it ain't broke, don't fix it."

As a leader, you're called to constantly look for opportunities to make things better. In many cases, this requires initiating and guiding groups and teams through adjustments. Leaders don't make changes for no reason, and any change you decide to make should be connected to the overall purpose or values of the team you're leading. Leaders must embrace the opportunity that positive change provides, and they should be courageous and bold enough to lead others through change, even when it's inconvenient or initially unwelcome.

If Moses were still alive on Earth, he could tell you all about change resistance. You would think Moses would have a lifelong approval rating through the roof after leading the Israelites out of Egyptian slavery and oppression. However, once Moses leads God's people out of captivity in Egypt and into the wilderness, it doesn't take long for discontentment and frustration to begin building. The Israelites constantly complain to Moses about their circumstances and openly pine for their days of slavery in Egypt.

There are a few dynamics going on here that are important to acknowledge. First of all, slavery in Egypt isn't better than wandering in the desert in the same way that being in prison isn't better than spending a day working at Dunder Mifflin, regardless of what Martin

Nash says. Secondly, this story reminds us of how hard it is to change. Change is unfamiliar. Change is uncertain. Pursuing change is like walking down a wilderness trail at night with only a small flashlight or lantern. And by the way, it's also raining. You may see far enough in front of you to know where you'll take your next few steps, but you certainly can't make out the destination.

Honestly, this isn't just a hypothetical situation for me. Over a semester in Texas, I worked at an internship called the Honor Academy. On a night when I was working security, we got word that one of the girls couldn't find her roommate. Meanwhile, the security booth received several reports from other interns who were receiving strange calls from a man with a voice that sounded like the serial killer from the movie "Scream." This was a concerning situation, to say the least.

We spread out through the campus to search for the girl. Coincidentally, we were outside in the middle of a rainstorm. We had flashlights, but because of the rain and the darkness, we could only see a few feet in front of us at a time.

Finally, we discovered the girl was in someone else's room, and the strange reported calls were coming from the boys' dorm. We quickly took their voice changer away and hoped that we wouldn't have a similar experience again.

Looking back on that night, I realize we had no idea what to do when danger presented itself, but we knew we needed to do something. Leadership is often the same way. As a leader, the path forward may not always be clear, but you know that you have to take the first step and trust that God will illuminate the rest of the path as you keep moving forward. Your motivation to keep going is a combination of faith as well as an awareness that standing in place or moving backward isn't a suitable option.

This is exactly what Moses did. When the people started complaining, Moses didn't turn around and lead the people back to Egypt even though that was what they wanted. Moses was willing to dig in his heels and continue charging toward the Promised Land. He wasn't perfect (read Numbers 20 if you don't believe me), but he kept his eye on the prize and rallied the people under his leadership around the belief that God was leading them to a better place than they had previously been.

Anyone who strives to be a leader will encounter situations where people are resistant to change. When this happens, what will you do? Will you give in to social pressure and pursue what's easy or convenient? Or will you live from conviction, willing to stick things out even in the face of opposition? Think back to our earlier conversation on motivation and consider whether you're willing to sacrifice some short-term discomfort or tension for the promise of long-term impact or influence.

Leaders are always growing

We talked about self-leadership in detail above, so we won't get too repetitive in this section. However, I must point out that the responsibility to continue growing and developing as a leader is never finished. You cannot give to someone else what you don't have yourself, and you'll never reach new heights as a leader unless you continue building your own character and leadership skills.

This is why Jesus constantly went away from the crowds (and even His closest disciples) to be by Himself and pray. It wasn't because Jesus didn't like people, and it certainly wasn't because He had to catch up on the release of His latest show or refresh His social media feed. Jesus understood that He couldn't pour from an empty cup.

This is especially critical in a world that tries to weigh us down with various pressures and different forms of stress. As Proverbs 11:25 (NLT) tells us, "The generous will prosper, those who refresh others will themselves be refreshed."

While this may sound like it runs against the grain of the advice that you typically hear, I think there's incredible truth and value in this message. Like you, I know what it's like to feel as though you have nothing left to give. Recently, I was in the middle of an especially difficult season. Somewhere in the middle of the storm, I unlocked a fresh approach that's made a massive difference.

What I learned is that the line between self-care and self-absorption or self-pity is razor-thin. If we spend too much time focusing on looking out for ourselves, we create a larger hole than the one we were first trying to escape. Rather than isolating ourselves in search of deeper levels of energy and fulfillment, we can find true refreshment by refreshing others. It's amazing how joy can exponentially multiply as we become more willing to freely give ourselves away in service of others.

Speaking of finding refreshment through connection, as you recognize the responsibility you have as a leader to continue to grow, you become more comfortable with embracing vulnerability as a tool to establish a greater connection with those you lead. There's a stigma of vulnerability that leads some leaders to shy away from being open about their struggles or limitations. Some people hear vulnerability and assume it means they must shed a lot of tears or expose every shortcoming from their past.

Not only is this an inaccurate perception of vulnerability, but it's also quite harmful. You don't need to share every good, bad, and ugly detail from your life so far in order to practice vulnerability. Instead, all you need to do in order to be vulnerable is acknowledge that you're not yet a finished product. Be open about the fact that you still have room to grow, and be specific about the areas where you're trying to improve. Chances are good that those around you can already see these limitations, and you'll build tremendous trust by acknowledging that you also know they are there.

A New Kind of Leader

Throughout this chapter, we've been speaking about leadership in a general way. However, there's still one big remaining question - how does our faith impact the way we lead? What sort of example does Jesus provide for us as a leader?

Okay, fine, two questions. But they are connected at the hip, and by addressing both of them, we'll find the secret sauce that makes our leadership truly impactful and transformational. In fact, it's such an important question that it needs its own chapter, which is exactly where we'll head next.

Application Questions

1. On a scale of one to ten, how would you rate your current ability to lead yourself? What would it take to raise your grade by 1-2 points?[8]
2. What's your attitude toward change? How can you better embrace change to help lead others through uncertainty?
3. How can you continue to grow as a leader? What steps will you take?

---

[8] If you're already at a ten, no need to answer the second question. However, I'd love to ask you a few questions and read the book you end up writing on leadership.

CHAPTER EIGHT:
LEADING WITH A SERVANT HEART

Be honest - when you were reading the last chapter, did you ever wonder why someone would want to lead if it's so challenging? After all, it doesn't exactly sound enjoyable. What's the point of leading or being a leader?

Ultimately, a leader is someone who is passionate about a particular cause and sees a better way of doing things. They choose to lead not because it's convenient or comfortable in the short term but because they want to see a future that looks different than the present. I would even argue that the best leaders are driven by a desire to make the world a better place for others to live in.

In other words, true and authentic leadership is not self-serving in the slightest. It's all about making a positive contribution to your family, church, organization, team, community, or society. And this is where it's incredibly helpful and valuable to look at the example Jesus sets for us as a leader.

Honestly, it's easy to take Jesus' leadership for granted as we become overly familiar with His life and story. It's easy to become desensitized to the stories we read in the Gospels if you grew up as a Christian or have been going to church for many years.

As we consider what it truly means to be a servant leader in light of Jesus' example, I hope that we can take a step back and read these stories with a fresh perspective in order to discover what's actually going on. I think this experience would be incredibly formational for us as we consider how we can effectively lead others. As Jesus teaches in Matthew 20:26-28 (NLT), "But among you it will be different. Whoever wants to be a leader among you must be your servant, and whoever wants to be first among you must become your slave [9]. For even the Son of Man came not to be served but to serve others and to give his life as a ransom for many."

All About Honor

Can you guess my two favorite jobs in the restaurant? I bet my answer will surprise you. More than anything else, I love doing dishes and cleaning in the dining room. I get so much joy from serving and doing the work that helps others. These tasks aren't especially glamorous or notable, but they enable me to remain humble while enhancing the experience for our guests and team members. It's easy to forget about the importance of clean dishes and a tidy dining room, but without them, our restaurant couldn't function.

The truth is that we can foster greater humility by doing the things most other people aren't willing to do. It also provides an incredible example to those around us. Can

---

[9] The Greek word used in the text (δοῦλος or "doulos") is sometimes translated as "servant" and sometimes translated as "slave" throughout the New Testament. Either way, it denotes a willful act and doesn't resemble forced slavery as we understand it today.

you imagine what my team members think when they see me, as the operator of the restaurant, washing dishes or picking up trash? It sends a message to the entire team about how seriously we value servant leadership and self-sacrifice.

I try to embody this posture because it's what I learn from the example of Jesus, and it truly brings me a sense of joy and satisfaction. In the ancient world, people cared deeply about receiving honor.[10] It's why the Pharisees and religious leaders felt so threatened by Jesus. They saw His teachings as a threat to their status and prestige and worried that Jesus' message might impact their standing in society.

Our world hasn't changed much in 2,000 years. To this day, many people view power, wealth, and fame as primary metrics of success. Some crave these accolades so strongly that they will do anything to accumulate more – even at the expense of others.

One of the things so intriguing about Jesus' story is His counterintuitive approach to honor and servant leadership. In Philippians 2 (a passage often referred to as "the Christ hymn"), Paul explains how Jesus abandoned His honorable position and took on the posture of a servant.

The striking contrast becomes even more apparent when you look at the original Greek language of the passage. Verse six says that Jesus was "μορφῇ Θεοῦ" (morphe Theou), or "in the same form as God", but verse seven emphasizes Jesus' decision to embrace μορφὴν δούλου

---

[10] https://www.unrv.com/book-review/empire-of-honor.php

(morphe doulou) or "the form of a servant". Jesus makes this transition in status by "emptying himself" or "making himself nothing" (depending on which translation you read).

This reminds me of the TV show "Undercover Boss," where CEOs and top organizational leaders go undercover to work in the lower levels of their company. This show is engaging because we don't expect to see people in power abandon their position in favor of a lower role.

Let us never forget that Jesus was the first "Undercover Boss." Not only did He empty Himself to embrace the nature of a servant, but He submitted Himself to a cruel death on a Roman cross (Philippians 2:8).

Jesus didn't just demote Himself to a lower level – He willingly gave up everything for the benefit of others. Through His self-sacrifice, God exalted Jesus to the highest place and seated Jesus at His right hand. Jesus humbled Himself to the lowest point imaginable, and God exalted Him to the highest possible place.

If we are going to practice authentic servant leadership, we must become people who can humbly value the wants and needs of others above our own. As the people of God, we have the power to change the world and bring God's kingdom to Earth as we follow Jesus' example. And it all starts with abandoning the desire for power and status and embracing a desire to serve others in love.

Repent to Begin

One of my favorite books is "Switch on Your Brain" by Dr. Caroline Leaf. In her book, Dr. Leaf argues that many of the illnesses that plague people today are a direct result of the quality of their thoughts. She uses scientific and medical research to show how we can achieve higher levels of health and wellness by simply altering our thought patterns. By flipping this "switch," we can live happier, healthier, and more enjoyable lives.

This switch is possible because of neuroplasticity. For many years, scientists believed we couldn't change thought patterns in our brains after they were developed. The common understanding was once you learned or believed something, it was impossible to change your mind. Neuroplasticity refers to our brain's ability to form new patterns of thought that are counterintuitive to what we believed previously.

While the scientific findings are less than 100 years old, this perspective actually supports a key principle from Jesus' ministry. If you're familiar with the Gospel message, you're well aware of Jesus' constant calls for people to repent. However, have you ever stopped to consider what it actually means to repent?

The original Greek word for repent was "metanoia," which, when translated literally, means to "change your mind" or "see things differently." This may catch you off guard if you're only used to hearing the word "repent" used in conjunction with sin. While the traditional connotations of repentance still make sense in light of this definition, we're also able to see repentance from another perspective with this refined understanding.

In my opinion, it makes Jesus' call to repentance even stronger. Think about it. Jesus wasn't just asking people to behave differently. He was challenging them to think in new ways. Since our thoughts and beliefs fuel our actions, this shift will still impact the way we behave. However, it also leads to a much deeper transformation.

If we're going to become true servant leaders, we must be willing to repent. We must change our minds. We must follow Paul's command in Romans 12:1 (NLT) after he tells us that offering our bodies as living sacrifices is the truest form of worship to God. He writes, "Don't copy the behavior and customs of this world, but let God transform you into a new person by changing the way you think. Then you will learn to know God's will for you, which is good and pleasing and perfect."

Some translations call this process the "renewing" of your mind. To me, this places a greater emphasis on the ongoing nature of this transformation. It's not a one-and-done action, but it's a process that we must continually pursue through regular practices such as daily prayer time in God's Word. In the same way that we're always cultivating our character garden and creating space for God to work, we must constantly take care of our minds to ensure we're focusing our thoughts and attention on God.

As we learn from Dr. Leaf's studies on transforming our brains, this is the best way to train ourselves to continually think differently. Paul supports this idea in the book of Philippians when he says, "And now, dear brothers and sisters, one final thing. Fix your thoughts on what is true, and honorable, and right, and pure, and lovely, and admirable. Think about things that are excellent and worthy of praise." (Philippians 4:8, NLT).

In short, we must change our minds to see leadership in new and fresh ways. It won't happen instantly, but through deliberate practice and a reliance on the Holy Spirit, we can train ourselves to see leadership as an activity of service to others and not as an opportunity to pursue selfish gain, power, or individual status.

What's cool about this process is that it forces you to trust in God. If we believe that God alone can transform hearts, we must submit to God's power as we work to create the prime environment for God to go to work. As Paul reminds us in 1 Corinthians 3:6, man can plant a seed, but God is the one who makes it grow. To bring back the garden illustration from Chapter Five, God is the one who will make our character grow, but we must be willing to do the work to create and maintain the garden. We can't force a tree to produce fruit, but we can do our part to create an ideal situation, tilling and fertilizing the soil, so to speak, where "seeds" are more likely to sprout and thrive.

Elevating Others through Servant Leadership

Have you ever found yourself in a scenario or situation you didn't feel like you were "good enough" to experience? Perhaps you usually fly coach, but one time, you received an upgrade and got to sit first class. Maybe you were invited to attend an event at a prestigious country club or an upscale restaurant and were blown away by the quality of the accommodations. Or you could have stayed for free at the Ritz Carlton in Laguna Beach with $600 worth of free clothing and a private One Republic concert.

That last one was highly specific and probably sounds made up, but it actually happened. A few years ago, my wife and I had an opportunity to go to Laguna Beach, California. We won a contest, and the prize was absolutely incredible. We stayed in a room overlooking the coast along a cliff.

When we arrived, they led us to a room where we could choose an extra pair of shoes and a light jacket or vest for our stay. Clothing from brands such as Patagonia, Lulu Lemon, and Olukai were all available for our choosing. Our choices alone were probably worth over $600. We immediately felt like royalty, and the feeling only intensified when we found ourselves at the final celebration singing along to "Counting Stars" and "Apologize" at our private performance.

When our surroundings or context exceeds our perceived value of ourselves, something strange and wonderful happens inside us. We feel grateful, privileged, and blessed. As followers of Jesus, we constantly have opportunities to experience this feeling. It's the defining aspect of our lives. Once we experience God's grace through Jesus, we enter a new reality where each day is a reminder of the good things we have that we don't deserve.

This is especially relevant in our conversation on leadership because it reminds us of the opportunity we have to use leadership not as a symbol of status or power but as a tool that can elevate the position or standing of others. One of my favorite illustrations of this concept is in 2 Samuel 9[11] after David officially succeeded Saul as king of Israel. In his early days as king, David captured the city of Jerusalem for Israel. He also enjoyed victories over the Philistines and brought the Ark of the Covenant back into Israelite possession.

Once things settled down, David wondered if anyone in Saul's family was still living because he wanted to show them kindness. At first glance, David's wish appears a little strange, as Saul repeatedly threatened David's life. However, David was close to Saul's son Jonathan before the Philistines took Jonathan's life, and David also showed Saul compassion and mercy on multiple occasions.

Word returned to David that Saul had a grandson, Mephibosheth, who was Jonathan's son. The first thing we learn about Mephibosheth is that he was lame in both feet (2 Samuel 9:3), meaning he couldn't walk. David sent one of his servants to bring Mephibosheth back into his presence.

I can only imagine how terrified Mephibosheth might have been when he heard the king wanted to see him. Perhaps he thought he was about to die. Consider how

---

[11]

https://www.biblegateway.com/passage/?search=2+Samuel+9&version=NLT

shocked he must have been to hear David's message in 2 Samuel 9:7 (NLT):

" 'Don't be afraid!' David said. 'I intend to show kindness to you because of my promise to your father, Jonathan. I will give you all the property that once belonged to your grandfather Saul, and you will eat here with me at the king's table!' "

"Mephibosheth bowed respectfully and exclaimed, 'Who is your servant, that you should show such kindness to a dead dog like me?' " (2 Samuel 9:8 NLT)

The Christian rock band Leeland summarizes this story from Mephibosheth's point of view in their song "Carried to the Table" from their 2006 album "The Sound of Melodies." The chorus of the song reads as follows:

> *"I was carried to the table*
> *Seated where I don't belong*
> *Carried to the table*
> *Swept away by His love*
> *And I don't see my brokenness anymore*
> *When I'm seated at the table of the Lord*
> *I'm carried to the table*
> *The table of the Lord"*

What a beautiful picture of God's grace manifested in a humble situation, not to mention a fantastic illustration of what it looks like to use leadership in a way that directly benefits others beyond ourselves.

Ultimately, I think that many of us are more like Mephibosheth than we realize. We received an invitation to the king's table, and Jesus carried us there through His sacrifice on the cross. Praise God for His extraordinary gift of salvation.

On the other hand, we can probably identify a few Mephibosheths in our lives. What if we're called to be David to those people? What could happen if we were willing to boldly step out as Christ-centered leaders empowered by the Holy Spirit and share God's grace and mercy with these people? What if you could be the one to carry that person to the table?

The Daily Cost of Leadership

Stories like Mephibosheth's are encouraging and uplifting, and they certainly provide us with a tremendous example worth repeating. However, we shouldn't fall into the trap of forgetting that servant leadership always comes with a cost.

In Luke 9:23, Jesus tells a large crowd that they must carry their cross each day to follow Him. While the cross evokes positive emotions (such as gratitude) from those familiar with Jesus' sacrifice and resurrection, it would have conveyed a different message to the people who first heard Jesus' words. It was a symbol of Roman oppression, torture, and death. It wasn't a symbol of victory or triumph. It was a physical manifestation of pain and suffering on the worst possible level.

Leadership is never a cakewalk, and if you're going to lead like Christ, you will definitely face your fair share of challenges and obstacles. The cost is substantial, and pain is guaranteed. How will you respond in times of adversity?

Application Questions

1. In what ways does your desire to honor others impact your leadership?
2. How can you continue to transform your mind so you can become the servant leader God has called you to be?
3. Who are 1-2 individuals or groups whom you could elevate through Christlike servant leadership?

CHAPTER NINE:
NAVIGATING CHALLENGES AND
OVERCOMING OBSTACLES

Ru Darby was three feet away from uncovering a large vein of gold that would be worth millions of dollars. Like many people, Darby was mining for gold during the years of the US Gold Rush. He originally found a large supply of gold in Colorado while working alongside his uncle, but the vein quickly disappeared. After spending much time and money trying to rediscover what they found originally, they walked away, and Darby became an insurance salesman.

They sold their equipment to a local man who became curious about the potential supply of gold underground. This man went back to where the Darbys had been digging and started working to uncover the gold himself. Not long after, he found the supply of gold that Darby and his uncle were so close to rediscovering. He ended up with the treasure that Darby never had.

Ultimately, Darby became very wealthy and successful himself, in part because of the impact of missing out on the gold. This experience was painful, but it taught him the value of persevering and never giving up. God has created each of us with enormous potential, but we won't stumble into this potential by accident.

If we're going to embrace the calling God has placed on our lives, we're going to have to learn how to keep moving in the face of obstacles and challenges. It won't be easy, but like each step so far in The Never-Ending Pursuit, there's as much value in the journey as there is in the destination.

Why do we face challenges?

If I had a compelling answer to this question, I wouldn't have waited until Chapter Nine to share it with you. People have been asking different forms of this question for thousands of years. "Why do bad things happen to good people?" "Why does evil exist in the world?" These questions aren't similar, but they reflect a similar frame of thinking.

Essentially, the belief is that if a good God created the world, it's hard to understand why any evil or negativity would exist alongside God's goodness. I'm not a professional theologian, so I won't attempt to answer this question in detail. I will say that God did not intend for it to be this way from the beginning. Sin messed things up when man chose sin over God.

Thankfully, God provided an escape from the grips of sin through His Son's sacrifice. As Paul tells us in 2 Corinthians 5:21 (NLT), "For God made Christ, who never sinned, to be the offering for our sin, so that we could be made right with God through Christ." All we must do to receive this free gift of salvation is believe in Jesus.

I praise God for this incredible gift while also recognizing that this doesn't fully resolve the fact that bad things still happen today. We can still make poor choices that lead to disastrous outcomes. God doesn't force these decisions on us, but it doesn't stop us from choosing sin. These choices cause the decay of creation and lead to disease.

We won't go too much deeper here, but I feel like a brief explanation is important to help us understand why we got here. What I can tell you, both from my understanding of Scripture as well as my personal experience, is that good things can come from bad situations, even if the events themselves cannot be described as "good." As we read in Romans 8:28 (NLT), "And we know that God causes everything to work together for the good of those who love God and are called according to his purpose for them."

One of my favorite verses in the entire Bible is in Romans 5. In the New Living Translation (NLT), verses 3-5 read: "We can rejoice, too, when we run into problems and trials, for we know that they help us develop endurance. And endurance develops strength of character, and character strengthens our confident hope of salvation. And this hope will not lead to disappointment. For we know how dearly God loves us, because he has given us the Holy Spirit to fill our hearts with his love."

The book of James begins with a similar message: "Dear brothers and sisters, when troubles of any kind come your way, consider it an opportunity for great joy. For you know that when your faith is tested, your endurance has a chance to grow. So let it grow, for when your endurance is fully developed, you will be perfect and complete, needing nothing" (James 1:2-4, NLT). James doesn't even open up with a joke or let his audience settle in before he tells them to change the way they think about trials and hard times.

To summarize, "Trials are good because they help you develop endurance, and that's all you need." The passage from Romans puts a cherry on top by connecting the development of endurance to the strengthening of our character (which we covered at length in Chapter Five) and reminding us that God still loves us even when we go through hard seasons.

That's no small matter, especially when you consider the dominant narrative at the time when the Bible was written. In Jesus' time, people believed life circumstances were directly correlated with a person's behavior or virtue. If you were wealthy and successful, you had favor in God's eyes. If you were poor, oppressed, or had a physical or mental illness, it was a sign that you (or your ancestors) had sinned. Think about John 9, where Jesus' disciples ask Jesus whose sin led to a man being born blind (see John 9:2), or the entire book of Job, where Job's friends repeatedly tell Job that his poor circumstances are a direct result of his wrongdoing.

Let me say this one more time because it bears repeating: God still loves us in the midst of trials and challenges. In the book "Grace is Greater," Kyle Idelman shares many stories of people going through tragedies I wouldn't wish on my worst enemies. He recounts people in his life who received life-altering medical diagnoses, lost young children, and experienced other unspeakable setbacks. What's surprising is that many of these people would tell you their faith actually grew stronger in these seasons. When you have nothing to hold onto but faith in God, your grip begins to tighten. Of course, we must keep our eyes focused on God when bad things happen and avoid the pull away from our faith.

This is the beauty of challenges and trials. Ultimately, I don't know why God allows bad things to happen. To be honest, there are times when I wish He wouldn't. I've seen tremendous hurt in the world, and it breaks my heart. At the same time, I'm thankful to serve a God who draws near to His people in their darkest hours. God's presence is often most tangible in our times of deepest need. We may not enjoy those feelings of grief, discomfort, and loss, but we know that we don't go through them alone.

In 2016, Oklahoma City Thunder assistant coach Monty Williams lost his wife, Ingrid, in a tragic car accident. She was only 44, and the couple had five children together. She sustained major injuries after being hit head-on by a car driving left of center at more than double the speed limit.

Less than ten days later, Monty stood up in front of a large crowd at Crossings Community Church in Oklahoma City to deliver his wife's eulogy. Despite his tremendous grief and the raw emotion of the moment, he put his faith on powerful display for everyone to see. He said the following during the speech: "This is hard for my family, but this will work out. And my wife would punch me if I were to sit up here and whine about what is going on. That doesn't take away the pain, but it will work out because God causes all things to work out. You just can't quit; you can't give in."

Later on, Williams would say, "Let us not forget that there were two people in this situation and that family needs prayer as well," Williams said. "And we have no ill will toward that family. That family didn't wake up wanting to hurt my wife. Life is hard -- it is very hard -- and that was tough. But we hold no ill will toward the Donaldson family."

The funeral took place on a Thursday afternoon. Later that evening, TNT's popular "Inside the NBA" show aired at its regular time. Instead of previewing the upcoming game or talking about current events around the league, the conversation focused on Williams's words and on faith. At one point, NBA Hall-of-Famer Charles Barkley remarked, "I don't know how anyone gets through hard times in life without faith."

That's simply beautiful. What an amazing testament to God's power and goodness, even in the worst possible moments.

As we lean into our faith despite the adversity we face, we experience profound development and tremendous growth. Our muscles don't grow stronger unless we first tear them down, and perseverance develops in a similar way. I think about the 2007 movie "Evan Almighty," a film starring Steve Carell and Morgan Freeman that imagines how the story of Noah's Ark might play out in the present day. At one point, Morgan Freeman (portraying God) asks

Evan's wife, "If someone prays for patience, you think God gives them patience? Or does he give them the opportunity to be patient? If he prayed for courage, does God give him courage, or does he give him opportunities to be courageous?"

God, in His infinite wisdom and power, did not make self-improvement easy. Oftentimes, the only way we can develop into the people we're supposed to be is by facing adversity head-on. Noah had to endure a once-in-a-lifetime flood. Abraham was called to leave behind the only home he ever knew and wait 25 years, until the age of 100, to have the child God promised him. Moses wandered until the Promised Land and never got in. David spent years running away from Saul, who wanted to kill him. If you find yourself in a storm, you're in good company.

I wish I could tell you why it was happening, but I'm confident that with the right approach, you can come out on the other side with stronger faith and greater endurance. And one day, you'll look back and be thankful for the goodness and richness the storm produced.

Stones of Remembrance

Like you, I've faced many challenges throughout my life, and I'm sure I'll experience more in the future. About a year ago, I had the opportunity to reflect on many of the ups and downs I've experienced throughout my life. I was headed home to see my dad and my former pastor. I planned to take my normal route but quickly learned about a major delay around Chicago and decided to take a detour to avoid the traffic.

I had no idea that I was about to embark on an incredible journey of introspection and gratitude. As I entered Pennsylvania, I began to travel down many of the same roads I had driven on many years before. Memories flooded my mind as I drove by my former college ministry house, my first apartment, and SonRise Church in Greensburg, PA, where I first served in ministry alongside one of my early youth pastors, Carl and his wife, Norma. For many years, I wanted to escape this place for all the hardship we suffered here. However, each location brought back incredible memories of times when I experienced God's faithfulness, even in the middle of hard seasons.

As I think about my experience, a question comes to mind. How do you want to remember this time in your life? You may be in the middle of a storm right now, and it might be hard to imagine what life will be like when the storm passes. Eventually, this time will come, and all that will be left behind are memories of what happened and how you responded. You don't have full control over what takes place, but you are responsible for choosing your response, and this matters more than you think.[12]

In 1 Samuel 6, the Israelites had just received the Ark of the Covenant back from Philistine captivity. They had lost control of the Ark sometime before in a battle where the Philistines killed over 30,000 Israelite soldiers (1 Samuel 4:10). After a strange series of events that included a Philistine idol falling on its face before the Ark on two

---

[12] Not trying to sound like a broken record, but I think this quote is once again relevant: "Life is 10% what happens to you and 90% how you respond."

separate occasions and the Lord sending plagues on the Philistine people shortly afterward, the Philistines decided they could no longer hold onto the Ark and returned it to the Israelites.

Samuel and the Israelites gathered together to commemorate the return of the Ark. While they were together, the Philistines pursued the Israelites once again, but God threw them into confusion, and Israel was victorious in battle. I'm sure this only intensified the celebration that was already underway.

Once the (second) battle was over, Samuel picked up a stone and placed it between Mizpah and Jeshanah. As we read in the second half of 1 Samuel 7:12 (NLT), "He named it Ebenezer (which means 'the stone of help'), for he said, 'Up to this point the Lord has helped us!' " Ironically, Ebenezer was also the name of the battleground where the Israelites had originally lost tens of thousands of soldiers, but because of God's provision, the name no longer had the same negative connotation. What was once a reminder of great loss was now a cause for celebration, an acknowledgment of God's great power and deliverance.

I'll give you another example of this concept in action. When you think of the cross, what comes to mind? If you're at all familiar with the story of Jesus, you probably feel positive emotions when you think of the cross. You obviously feel somber as you think about Jesus' pain and sacrifice on the cross, but you feel great joy when you think about Jesus' eventual resurrection and the path Jesus paves for us to experience the same new life in salvation.

In the ancient world, the cross would have conveyed a much different message. The cross was a symbol of grotesque torture and Roman dominance. It was a punishment reserved for the worst of criminals – usually terrorists and anyone who threatened the power of the Roman regime. It's this exact stigma that makes Jesus' willingness to suffer death on the cross so shocking while also making the reversal of the general perception of a cross all the more powerful.

I imagine you have some stones of remembrance as well. These stones are reminders of negative circumstances or difficult seasons in life that now remind you of God's provision and protection. As you reflect on these "stones," you remember how God gave you the power and support you needed to overcome hard seasons, and you're reminded that if God can do it once, He can do it again. You also develop the courage you need to embrace hard seasons rather than avoid them.

The Storms that Define Us

Have you ever seen the movie "The Money Pit?" I feel like I've lived out the plot of that movie over the last five years. I'm so thankful we have a house, but I can't understate how challenging it's been to keep up with all the hidden problems that weren't disclosed to us during the home inspection.

One time, we had to replace old outlets in the living room. Initially, we thought the job would cost a few hundred dollars. Seven thousand dollars later, I felt like I had whiplash. It turns out that the old owners had attempted to fix the melted main wire with some electrical tape. The wire became brittle and led to an emergency situation that required us to replace the whole panel box.

There are a few important takeaways from this story. First of all, while electrical tape is good in many situations, it's not an appropriate fix for a melted wire. More importantly, as Taylor Swift once taught us, band-aids don't fix bullet holes. [13] You can't sweep things under the rug and expect them to go away. You must be willing to acknowledge your challenges and deal with them head-on if you're ever going to move forward in life.

My favorite movie of all time is *The Count of Monte Cristo*. In the movie, the Count is giving a birthday toast to his sworn enemy's "son," Albert. Later on in the movie, the Count discovers Albert is actually his son in a strange turn of events. Seriously, it's so great, and you need to watch it if you haven't already seen it.

Anyways, during his toast, the Count says, "Life is a storm, my young friend. You'll bask in the sunlight one moment, be shattered on the rocks the next. What makes you a man is what you do when that storm comes. You must look into that storm and shout as you did in Rome. Do your worst, for I will do mine! Then the fates will know you as we know you: as Albert Mondego, the man!"

In other words, the storms we face in life are what make us who we are. How will your storms define you? How will you respond to the storms in life so that you can come out better, faster, and stronger on the other side? Take the Count's advice, stare your storm in the face, and give it

---

[13] If you don't get this reference, we have bad blood. Just kidding. I like you, partially because you've read this far.

everything you've got. You may not feel like you have what it takes, but trust in God to fill in the gaps and give you whatever you need to keep moving forward in the face of uncertainty.

It's not about you

By now, we've established that challenges are inevitable and, in some cases, beneficial. At the same time, I don't think they will ever become enjoyable. [14] While we can't expect to find extreme pleasure or fun challenges, we can do some preparation ahead of time to lessen the discomfort.

Understanding that challenges are inevitable is a great start. It's also wise to think about how we go about framing certain experiences as challenges and whether or not that's the best perspective. Remember, you can always choose your attitude and adjust your expectations.

Think about a toddler who's just been told they won't get dessert after dinner. With the wrong perspective, that feels like the worst thing that could ever happen to anyone. However, the real challenge is not the event itself but the interpretation of the event.

You can't blame a toddler for acting this way because they don't know any better yet, but you can think critically about how you process things that happen in your life and whether or not you could think differently about what's going on. If you're able to develop this skill, you may find

---

[14] Perhaps one day I will enjoy them, but I haven't grown enough to get to this place... yet.

that some of your most common "challenges" are really only minor inconveniences.

For example, a long line at the grocery store is not a challenge. Your favorite college football team losing is not a challenge. Chick-fil-A taking cole slaw off the menu is not a challenge. [15] Anyways, you may not enjoy these experiences, but you can reframe them so that they don't distract you from more important pursuits.

At the heart of this mental transformation is accepting the fact that life is not about you. When you're not living selfishly, you find yourself caring less about how things impact you and more about how they affect others. You'll experience far less of these meaningless so-called "challenges," and the obstacles you do face will be higher-leverage issues that impact more people than just you.

The Missing Ingredient

We've talked about the value of challenges. We've discussed how you can find stones of remembrance that remind you of God's power over life's greatest storms. We've even considered how we can reframe challenges so that they don't have as great an impact on you. There's still one element missing that will forever change the way you approach challenges, and I've intentionally saved it for last.

---

[15] Actually, that one is pretty real. Sorry to bring up a sore subject.

Application Questions

1. What challenges have you faced in life that were deeply formational? What are your "stones of remembrance?"
2. How can you embrace challenges as opportunities to grow and develop? What will you need to do differently?
3. What's an everyday challenge you face that you could reframe so you aren't distracted from more important matters?

CHAPTER TEN:
BUILDING POSITIVE RELATIONSHIPS

For many weeks, "Ted Lasso" was the number-one streaming show on Apple TV. The show was watched for over 700 million minutes during the last week of April 2023. The show humorously depicts Ted Lasso's (played by Jason Sudeikis) journey from a mid-level American football coach to becoming the manager of a Premier League English football (soccer) club.

The only problem was that Ted Lasso knew nothing about the sport most people around the world call football, and the team suffered relegation during his first year as coach. By this point, Ted had built a strong rapport with his players, so he still had the support of the locker room. After the final game of the season, Ted stands up to speak to his players. He acknowledges their sadness at the outcome of the season, but he reminds them of the one thing worse than being sad: being alone. He then assures each player that none of them are alone.

Admittedly, our approach throughout most of this book has been largely individual. You can determine your purpose, choose your values, set goals, and build character mostly on your own. Sure, there are some elements of leadership that involve other people, but the scale still leans heavily on the side of an individual (and not a communal) pursuit. This is all about to change because we can't understate the impact of strong relationships in virtually everything we do.

The power of community

The cadence of the creation story in Genesis 1-2 is stunningly beautiful. God creates the world by speaking things into existence. Each time God creates, God calls His creation "good." The process repeats several times over until we reach a strange twist in the story. All of a sudden, something is "not good."

If you're familiar with the story, you already know what I'm referring to. God establishes light and darkness, distinguishes the sky from the ground, and separates the water from the dry land on Earth. He fills the sky with planets and stars, fills the world with plants and animals, and caps off creation by creating a man in His own likeness. The world is beautiful, with one small exception: "Then the Lord God said, 'It is not good for the man to be alone. I will make a helper who is just right for him.' " (Genesis 2:18, NLT)

In its earliest form, the world was good. The only thing it was missing was relationships. God didn't make man to exist in isolation. God created people to live with and for each other.

This concept is especially relevant in many parts of the world outside the United States. I live in the United States of America, and many of you probably do as well. Americans tend to be highly individualized as a product of the culture we live in. Some countries throughout the world are similar, but many are not. In fact, if you travel to certain parts of Africa, Asia, Central America, and elsewhere in the world, you'll find that many people have a highly communal sense of their identity. They aren't defined as an individual person. They understand themselves largely in light of their family, village, or town.

Regardless of what part of the world you live in, I can't overstate the importance of community and relationships. You could write multiple books on the role of relationships in our lives, and I almost feel like I'm doing a disservice by trying to condense an entire conversation on relationships into one chapter. However, when I think about the impact of relationships on our lives, three things immediately come to mind:

- Relationships give us a practical opportunity to share the love we receive from God.
- Relationships provide tremendous joy.
- Relationships should make us better.

Let's dive deeper into each of these benefits with Proverbs 27:17 (NLT) in mind: "As iron sharpens iron, so a friend sharpens a friend."

"We love because Christ first loved us"

The night before Jesus goes to the cross, He gives a speech to His disciples that many scholars refer to as the "Farewell Discourse." He shares these words with His disciples when they gather for the Passover meal and after He washes each disciple's feet Himself. Early in this speech, Jesus gives His disciples a challenge. He says, "So now I am giving you a new commandment: Love each other. Just as I have loved you, you should love each other." (John 13:34, NLT). John later reinforces this idea in 1 John, saying, "We love each other because he loved us first" (1 John 4:19, NLT).

Jesus wants His disciples to share the love He's given them with people everywhere, knowing that this is the only way to undo the damage of sin and evil in the world. He understands that as we experience the powerful and transformational love of our Creator, reflecting this love to the world around us is the only natural response.

In some ways, love is hard to define. Many people's initial impression is that love is a feeling. Cory Matthews didn't help this misunderstanding when he described his feelings for Topanga on an episode of "Boy Meets World" by saying he knew he loved her because "he felt better when he was around her." While this is often a byproduct of love, it's not the genesis of love, either.

We must reject the idea that love is primarily a feeling and embrace the understanding of love as a decision and a commitment. If we prioritize the feeling of love rather than the decision to act in love, it will be too easy to give up when those feelings are hard to perceive. We're hardwired to serve and sustain ourselves, but love often requires us to empty ourselves for the benefit of others. With Jesus as our example and as the one who first loved us in this way by emptying Himself on the cross, we take on the challenge to share love even when it's hard.

We work hard to embody this model of love in our restaurant. At our Chick-fil-A in West Des Moines, we make various promises to all our team members when they come on board. We remind them that we don't have all the answers to each problem, but we commit to responding in a certain way when team members experience trials of different kinds. I believe this framework is at the heart of developing strong relationships with each of our valued employees.

First, we invest in each team member. We provide one-on-one development with leaders and ongoing training in group sessions. These lessons don't just benefit our employees during the time they work in our restaurant, but they translate into life skills that are useful in any field. We care deeply about helping our employees reach their personal goals, and this is one way that we put this value into action.

Next, we commit to listening. Even when we don't have specific answers or advice, we can always listen to what other people have to say. No matter how hard life gets, we will always come alongside each of our team members with a promise to help carry the burdens they must lift until they can see the light at the end of the tunnel. In addition, we listen carefully to feedback to ensure we meet employee's expectations, and we even compensate employees who bring great ideas to the table.

Finally, we always take care of our team. We offer tremendous benefits and reward employees early and often for their hard work. We give regular rewards to employees through our "Cluck Buck" system, and we allow employees to "Level Up" before their regular reviews if they are consistently performing above expectations. We want employees to develop, and we're always looking for ways to honor and celebrate employees who go above and beyond.

We believe in carrying out these principles regardless of a person's race, culture, faith, upbringing, ethnicity, or socioeconomic class. These aren't the factors that give a person a sense of worth. It's true that these things help build identity and character. However, each person has value simply because they were created by God and in the image of God. This is what our founding fathers were referring to when they wrote in the Declaration of Independence, "We hold these truths to be self-evident, that all men are created equal, that they are endowed by their Creator with certain unalienable Rights." We believe that nobody should ever have to live with uncertainty about the future because God has a plan for what lies ahead, and we'll do our part to make these plans come into reality.

When we show love in this way, we foster environments that reflect the second major principle of relationships: relationships provide tremendous joy.

Life is better together

Like many people, I spent the first part of my life believing I could do everything on my own. More often than not, this approach left me feeling burned out and frustrated. There were simply too many fires to put out, too many balls to keep in the air, and too many plates to keep spinning at one time.

I was constantly irritated. I shut myself off from others, and I would snap at my wife and children out of frustration. I reached a point where I couldn't take it anymore and decided something had to give. As I once heard a pastor say, "You'll never move from 'here' to 'there' until 'here' becomes completely unacceptable."

I started by opening up to my wife about what I was feeling and asking for prayer. Next, I sought advice from one of my pastors. I began to see that I needed to rely on the support of those whom I had hired. They were ready to help me carry the burden, but I had to allow them. My own strength might be limited, but when I had others working alongside me, I was capable of so much more.

During this season, I had an incredible epiphany while reading "The Power of the Other" by Dr. Henry Cloud. In his book, Dr. Cloud says, "People trying to reach goals succeed at a much greater rate if they are connected to a strong human support system." He also explains how Navy Seals are able to push themselves far beyond typical physical limitations because they are working alongside others. When they harness "the power of the other," they find a deeper source of strength to push themselves to new heights.

At first glance, it seems borderline supernatural. When we look through the lens of faith, we begin to recognize what's really taking place. As the Teacher says in Ecclesiastes 4:12 (NLT), "A person standing alone can be attacked and defeated, but two can stand back-to-back and conquer. Three are even better, for a triple-braided cord is not easily broken."

Life is better lived with other people for several reasons. First of all, there's a sense of joy that comes from our most important relationships that nothing else this side of Heaven can match. This obviously begins with our relationship with God but continues on into our family relationships and key friendships. Few things bring me more joy than date nights with my wife (it probably won't surprise you that a couple who's owned multiple restaurants are 100% foodies), beach trips with my family (even in the pouring rain), and maintaining connections over several decades with friends who have seen me at my best and my worst, but choose to love and support me anyways.

In addition, our relationships are a source of fuel that can push us to new heights when we surround ourselves with people who have strong values and character. These are the people who encourage us, challenge us, and bring out the best in us. I haven't always surrounded myself with these kinds of people, but once I recognized how important it was, I never looked back.

"Show me your friends, and I'll show you your future."

Early in my life, I spent a lot of time hanging around the wrong crowd. It didn't take long before their actions and beliefs began to influence my own behaviors. I'm not blaming them because they weren't telling me what to do. However, it certainly didn't help that we all wanted to do the wrong things. At no point did anyone stop to question our decisions or suggest a better way.

Later on, I started attending church again and spending more time with my youth group. I began making new friends who had different values and wanted to see me live the best possible life according to God's plan. Even though I was losing some of my old "friends", I was now in a much healthier friend circle, and it made a massive difference in the way I lived my life.

Life is certainly better with others, but only when we put the right people around us who can produce this type of effect in our lives. Jim Rohn once said that each person is the average of the five people they spend the most time with. Similarly, Dan Pena was quoted as saying, "Show me your friends and I'll show you your future." The premise of both quotes is the same: Our closest relationships play a critical role in shaping who we are, both in the present and in the future.

This is why children often take on the personality and tendencies of their parents. It's why you may notice yourself talking like your friends or slowly becoming more like your spouse as you spend more years together. The psychological term is "social influence," and it refers to the invisible force that leads us to think, talk, or act a certain way in order to fit in with a group. If we're unaware that this force exists, it can be dangerous. On the other hand, if we acknowledge what's taking place, we can carefully choose our friends and peers based on the type of life we ultimately want to live.

In short, we must think about the role other people play in our journey to lifelong faithfulness and ultimate impact. Are we surrounding ourselves with people who have similar values and goals that we do? Are they supporting us on our journey? Are they challenging us to be the best versions of ourselves while also helping to unearth the potential inside us that we may not even see yet?

How do we know when it's time to end a relationship?

If you follow the principles in this chapter, you'll experience the beauty of fulfilling, life-giving relationships. However, relationships are a joint effort, and there may be times when someone else isn't willing to do their share. If a person in your life isn't pointing you closer to Christ or supporting your ongoing transformation and growth, it may be best if you don't invest significant time and energy into that relationship.

Henry Cloud discusses this concept at length in another one of his books, "Necessary Endings." Cloud writes, "Without the ability to end things, people stay stuck, never becoming who they are meant to be, never accomplishing all that their talents and abilities should afford them." To put it bluntly, if you care about achieving your potential and growing into the person God has called you to be, you'll need to learn how to close some doors, stop some bad habits, and, yes, end some relationships.

If you're truly the average of the five people you spend the most time with, you want your key relationships to be with people who not only give you joy but also make you better. Of course, if you find that somebody is encouraging you to do things that are sinful or immoral, it's easy to know when it's time to cut this person out. You can make this shift away from people without being rude or dehumanizing them. There's a difference between being assertive and aggressive.

Part of being assertive is clarifying your needs and values and explaining how they factor into whatever decision you are making. Say you have a friend who always wants to get together and gossip about others. You know that Scripture speaks out against gossiping, and you want to eliminate as much gossip from your life as possible. You tell your friend that you prefer not to gossip about others in your conversations and that you won't engage in this kind of talk.

By doing this, you aren't challenging their character or demeaning their personhood. You're simply stating a personal boundary. Brene Brown describes setting boundaries as a process of stating what is acceptable and unacceptable. For example, "It's OK for us to spend time together and talk about what's going on in our lives. It's not OK for us to talk badly about people behind their backs."

Once you set clear boundaries and make your preferences and values known, you've done your part. Unfortunately, you can't control how the other person responds. Their reaction may dictate the future of the relationship. If they accept what you have to say and respect your boundaries, the relationship might be able to continue in some capacity. On the other hand, if they continue to toe the line or put you in situations where you're not comfortable, it might be a sign that it's time for the relationship to end.

This isn't because relationships are meant to be self-serving, but because, as we learn from 1 Corinthians, "bad company corrupts good character" (1 Corinthians 15:33, NLT). Ultimately, the goal of our relationships is to provide us with opportunities to express the love of Christ and be encouraged and challenged to grow our faith. If we're participating in relationships that don't fulfill both these goals, they are deadweights that hold us back from our Never-Ending Pursuit and our potential.

True Greatness is Consistency

We've come a long way since we first began our journey. We've covered important topics like discovering your purpose, defining your values, and setting compelling goals for the future. We've discussed building character, cultivating strong leadership, and approaching challenges and obstacles with faith and a growth mentality. If you can commit to consistently doing these things at a high level, you will flourish in life and leave a lasting positive impact.

I don't use the word "consistency" lightly. Without consistency, you're a one-hit wonder. Consistency is what turns a sprint into a marathon. I don't want you to run a few laps and call it a day. I want you to be fully equipped for the long haul. I want you to have the same experience Paul describes when he says, "I have fought the good fight, I have finished the race, and I have remained faithful. And now the prize awaits me—the crown of righteousness, which the Lord, the righteous Judge, will give me on the day of his return. And the prize is not just for me but for all who eagerly look forward to his appearing." (2 Timothy 4:7-8, NLT). In the words of James Clear, "True greatness is consistency."

So before we wrap this book up, I want to make sure you have all the tools you need to sustain the growth and development we've shown you to this point. I want you to learn what it means to "abide" in the next chapter. I want you to see what it looks like to follow this path, not just for a few days or weeks, but for years to come.

Application Questions

1. What tasks or obligations are you trying to handle alone that could be easier if you shared them with others?
2. What relationships have the greatest impact on your life? What difference do those relationships make, and how could you benefit from investing more time in these relationships?
3. Think about your ideal future. What types of relationships do you need to have in order to get where you want to go?

CHAPTER ELEVEN:
SUSTAINING GROWTH AND
TRANSFORMATION

You've probably heard the saying, "Slow and steady wins the race." I'm not entirely sure where it comes from, but I'm sure the ancient fable of the tortoise and the hare has something to do with it.

If it's been a while since you've read the full story or if you've only ever heard it in passing, I'll briefly explain what happens. The folktale begins with the rabbit challenging the turtle. The hare asks the turtle mockingly, "Do you ever get anywhere?" The turtle responds confidently: "Yes, and I get there faster than you think. Let's run a race, and I'll prove it."

The race begins with the hare speeding ahead of the tortoise. Once the tortoise is out of sight, the hare decides to further humiliate the tortoise by laying down beside the course to take a nap. The tortoise kept moving, slowly but steadily, until he passed the hare on the path. The hare continued to sleep while the tortoise got closer to the finish line. Eventually, the hare woke up, but it was too late. Even with an all-out sprint, he still couldn't make up enough ground before the turtle finished the race ahead of him.

We like this story because it makes us feel like anything is possible. *I don't have to be a rabbit to win the race. I can run at a turtle's pace and still come in first!* While this is a great takeaway, there's also an inherent challenge that we must notice as well. Just like the turtle never stopped moving in pursuit of the finish line, we must continue to make consistent progress in our own pursuit as well. You can win a 100-meter dash with a sprint, but you'll never complete an ultramarathon if you can't figure out how to pace yourself and continue gaining traction even when you get tired.

If we're going to keep moving forward in our Never-Ending Pursuit without breaking down or giving in, we'll have to learn how to carefully plan our steps, find opportunities for rest and rejuvenation, and develop perseverance along the way. We must know how to show up and keep pushing even when we don't feel like it. We must follow Jesus' example by picking up our cross daily.

Taking Up Your Cross

There's a moment in Jesus' life where the dominant narrative begins to change. From the moment Jesus began His ministry, people could sense that something was different about Him. He wasn't just another prophet, but He was someone who spoke with a palpable authority (see Mark 1:27). He attracted large crowds, healed the sick, drove out demons, fed crowds, and captivated audiences. People were intrigued by Jesus, and the question they couldn't stop asking was, who exactly is this man?

Jesus knows what the people are thinking and chooses to address the topic while alone with His disciples. As we read in Mark 8:27-28 (NLT), "Jesus and his disciples left Galilee and went up to the villages near Caesarea Philippi. As they were walking along, he asked them, 'Who do people say I am?' 'Well,' they replied, 'some say John the Baptist, some say Elijah, and others say you are one of the other prophets.'"

Quick note - we shouldn't be surprised that people commonly identified with Jesus with somebody prominent from their past. When our brains can't comprehend something new and different, we try to make sense of it by comparing it to something familiar. It's a natural response, even if it's inaccurate in this particular circumstance.

Jesus can sense there's more the disciples aren't saying, and He knows the right answer hasn't yet been shared. So he probes a little deeper, saying, "But who do you say I am?" (Mark 8:29) It's interesting that the disciples' initial reaction was to answer on behalf of someone else and not to share their own thoughts, but we can always trust Peter to act on impulse (for better or for worse). Peter replied, "You are the Messiah."

We must acknowledge that we interpret the word "Messiah" much differently than the disciples would have. To us, we can't separate our understanding of the Messiah apart from Jesus. If you've grown up in the Church, it's been ingrained in your head from the time you were sipping fruit punch and eating goldfish while watching your VBS teacher place characters on a flannelgraph (or, if you were born after the year 1990, while watching Veggie Tales).

For the Israelites who lived during the time period when Jesus walked the Earth, the word "Messiah" had much stronger political undertones. To Peter, Andrew, James, John, and the rest of Jesus' disciples, the Messiah was the "Anointed One" who would restore the kingdom of Israel and deliver the nation from Roman captivity. The arrival of the Messiah would mean the establishment of a new kingdom unlike any the world had ever seen.

Ultimately, this is exactly what happens, but certainly not in the way the disciples expected. Jesus wouldn't become king without first carrying a cross and wearing a crown of thorns. He knows what lies ahead at this point in time, but His disciples don't, which is probably why His response to Peter's declaration is so shocking:

> *"But Jesus warned them not to tell anyone about him.*
>
> *Then Jesus began to tell them that the Son of Man must suffer many terrible things and be rejected by the elders, the leading priests, and the teachers of religious law. He would be killed, but three days later he would rise from the dead.*
>
> *As he talked about this openly with his disciples, Peter took him aside and began to reprimand him for saying such things.*
>
> *Jesus turned around and looked at his disciples, then reprimanded Peter. 'Get away from me,*

Satan!' he said. 'You are seeing things merely from a human point of view, not from God's.'

Then, calling the crowd to join his disciples, he said, 'If any of you wants to be my follower, you must give up your own way, take up your cross, and follow me.'"

Mark 8:30-34, NLT

Talk about a plot twist. The disciples thought Jesus was on a one-way street to success, power, wealth, and influence, and they were going to be along for the ride. Instead, Jesus takes the sharp turn that nobody was expecting by bringing together two concepts that nobody in their wildest dreams would have paired together beforehand: glory and suffering.

To Jesus, being the Messiah wasn't about a crown but about a cross. In fact, Jesus resisted earlier attempts from men who wanted to make Him king by force (see John 6:14-15). His goals were much different and much bigger than establishing a new earthly kingdom.

The implications of Jesus' revamped understanding of honor and glory extend to Jesus' followers as well. Jesus isn't just interested in an individual pursuit – He wants to begin a new movement. This is why, after reprimanding Peter for suggesting a different approach, He stresses the importance of constant sacrifice and surrender to His disciples. Jesus' calling on our lives requires us to deny ourselves, pick up our cross, and follow the path that Jesus walked before us. I like the extra detail Luke adds to this story, including the word "daily" when sharing Jesus' command to take up our cross (see Luke 9:23).

As we consider what it looks like to pursue a life grounded in goodness, righteousness, and continual growth, we can't ignore the tremendous responsibility of consistency that Jesus calls us to embody. We can't run the race like the hare, who sprints for a while before stopping to nap beside the road.

Instead, we have to run like the turtle. We may not always travel at breakneck speeds, but we're committed to making gradual progress and never stopping. We embody what Paul writes in Galatians 6:9 (NLT) when he says, "So let's not get tired of doing what is good. At just the right time we will reap a harvest of blessing if we don't give up."

We also have to remember that this calling won't always be easy to pursue. If Jesus experienced great suffering in His life, it's foolish for us, as His followers, to believe we will experience anything different. However, we find great hope and promise in our calling that energizes us to persist despite these setbacks and heartbreaks. As Jesus tells His disciples in John 16:33 (NLT), "Here on earth you will have many trials and sorrows. But take heart, because I have overcome the world."

This encouragement comes at the end of Jesus' Farewell Discourse, which we discussed in the last chapter. There's another nugget in that speech that I can't ignore when I think about what it means to continually pursue growth and development in Christ. It means so much to me that I spent hundreds of hours and thousands of dollars alongside a few close friends to create a program that would help people understand and apply this key teaching.

The impact of "abiding"

Few (if any) men have had as significant an impact on me as my friend and former pastor, Shawn Lyons. I admire how Pastor Shawn has overcome challenges throughout his life as he's pursued God's calling. Shawn struggled with various physical challenges (in addition to a learning disability) throughout his childhood. However, everything changed when Pastor Shawn heard the truth about Jesus at age 12 and felt a calling to preach God's word. Pastor Shawn has spent the last 37 years ministering in different churches and sharing boldly about Jesus's impact on his life.

I remember the first time I heard Pastor Shawn speak about the "Abide Factor," based on Jesus' words to His disciples in John 15. This powerful concept immediately struck me. The word "abide" means to dwell, be present, or remain. To abide in Christ requires letting go of the past and focusing on our future growth and transformation in Christ. Life isn't always easy or predictable, but if we can develop a greater understanding of what it means to abide in Christ, we find all the tools we need to live out our faith and stay grounded no matter what happens to us.

I began spending time with Pastor Shawn and Nate, his son-in-law, to further discuss the concept of abiding. These conversations led to the development of "The Abide Factor: A Biblically-based approach to living an abundant life and bearing fruit in Christ," which you can purchase on Amazon or wherever books are sold. We also created a mentorship program to help people break free from their struggles and learn how to pursue a life grounded in the teachings of Jesus. You can learn more at www.provenresultsmentors.com.

In *The Abide Factor* book, Pastor Shawn dives much deeper into the specifics of what it means to "abide," but here's a quick overview:

- **Abide.** Abiding in Jesus requires us to stay when it would be easier to walk away. We may not know what challenges lie ahead, but we choose to live out our faith despite the obstacles we face.
- **Bless.** We bless God through worship, service, and regular time spent in prayer and the Word.
- **Incline.** As you prioritize your faith and allow God to transform your heart and mind, you begin to see the world from a new perspective, and you find your thoughts and actions more closely resembling what Jesus would do.
- **Dwell.** To dwell in God's presence means maintaining a constant awareness of the role God plays in your life. God is the ultimate source of protection, help, and guidance, both in the good seasons and the bad seasons.
- **Everything.** Because our faith is our overarching identity, we must be willing to surrender everything to Jesus and seek first His kingdom (see Matthew 6:33).

While it's not always easy to live this way, it's what Jesus calls us to pursue, and it has the power to transform our minds and spirits completely – but only if we commit to abide on a regular basis. These principles don't work if we only pick them up every once in a while. They must be practiced, refined, and, ultimately, become habitual.

The value of sticking it out

As you develop a "tortoise" mindset and learn how to abide in Jesus and take up your cross daily, you'll grow stronger over time, and you'll find it easier to continue on your pursuit. At the same time, you're not on a solo journey. Your mission involves other people as well. Remember what you learned in Chapter Ten: life is better when we live with other people. At the same time, interpersonal conflicts can knock us off course and derail our pursuit when we don't know how to properly engage with people in the midst of disagreements or tension.

Regardless of where you live and work, you're going to face conflict with other people. This isn't even a bad thing. When approached properly, conflict can be a tremendous opportunity for growth. What makes conflict dangerous is not its existence but our tendency to avoid conflict or approach it with an improper attitude. Too many people are more interested in attacking the person who is causing the conflict rather than attempting to resolve the issue at hand. This is just as dangerous (if not more harmful) than ignoring the conflict or running away.

When I was younger, I worked at a juvenile delinquent facility in the Appalachian Mountains. This program was designed to help troubled young people deal with their problems through an experimental outdoor approach. I felt like it was just as challenging for me as it was for anyone else there. If you weren't being attacked physically or emotionally by the students, you were worn down from the daily physical labor.

I badly wanted to quit. I was required to be there seven days out of every two weeks, and I missed my normal life at home. Every day, I woke up and wanted to leave. However, for the first time in my life, I chose not to run from the struggle. I worked in the program for almost four years. I'd be lying if I told you I ever wanted to go back and do it again, but I also regard this period as one of the most influential and rewarding times in my entire life. I learned the value of not discarding or ignoring difficult people, and I gained practical experience in loving and working with others in spite of our differences.

This season in my life taught me about the value of sticking out a hard situation, even when it didn't feel like something I wanted to do. If you're going to pursue sustainable growth and transformation, the ability to stay with something that isn't enjoyable will be invaluable. It's the only way that you can expect to take meaningful steps toward excellence.

Excellence as the Only Standard

I love the way Truett Cathy talked about excellence as the highest possible standard. He used to say, "Success is a temporary arrangement, but excellence endures when success moves on." In other words, when we can define what excellence looks like in our lives and see where we are in relation to the standard, we can identify the gap between where we are and where we want to be. From there, we can set up basecamps or guideposts along the way that help us track our progress and stay on track toward achieving our goals.

Speaking of goals, here's another one of my favorite Truett Cathy quotes: "No goal is too high if we climb with care and confidence." Excellence can't happen overnight, but if you commit to long-term growth and perseverance, no goal is too high.

In other words, the thought of maintaining your pursuit from this point on may feel overwhelming, but you'll be motivated to keep moving when you have a goal in sight. You'll never achieve perfection, and neither will I – at least not in this lifetime. Jesus is the only One who could ever reach this standard on Earth. However, when we make excellence our goal, we'll be willing to do the hard work of self-improvement, and we'll always be looking to do more and be more than what we are today.

The impact of this pursuit won't just benefit us. It will also have an effect on our families, our workplaces, our churches, our communities, and, potentially, the world as a whole. Truthfully, that's what this whole book has been about. I'm not only interested in helping you, but I want to pass along what I've learned in a way that produces an impact in you that transcends your life and bleeds into everything you touch. Like a pebble in a pond that creates a ripple effect far beyond its initial point of contact, I believe God will do amazing things through you to bless and enrich others' lives if you take these words seriously and work to put them into practice.

Application Questions

1. Practically speaking, what does it look like for you to "take up your cross" each day?
2. What element of The Abide Factor could make the biggest impact in your life? Which aspect is the hardest for you to apply?
3. If you could develop enough perseverance to stick it out through hard seasons, how would it impact your life (and the lives of the people closest to you)?

CONCLUSION: MAKING IT STICK

Before the days of Christmas movies like *Elf* and *Christmas Story*, we watched classics like *Santa Claus is Comin' to Town* each holiday season. It's not quite as old as *It's a Wonderful Life*, but it came out more than 50 years ago (I felt so old typing that sentence). The animated movie is narrated by Fred Astaire and tells the story of how Santa Claus and several other Christmas traditions came about.

At one point in the movie, Kris Kringle is headed back to his adopted family with Topper, a lost penguin he befriended while on a trip to Sombertown to deliver toys. Along the way, they are captured by the Winter Warlock, but Kris gives the Winter Warlock a toy and his hard exterior melts away.

After this, the Warlock and Kris become friends, and the Warlock starts to wonder if he could leave his evil ways behind and change. He likes the idea of living differently, but isn't sure if it's possible. He tells Kris, "I really am a mean and despicable creature at heart, you know. It's so difficult to really change."

Let's pause here before I tell you what happens next (some of you can already sense the song coming). Can you relate? Have you ever felt like the Winter Warlock? Have you ever wondered if you could truly change or if you'll always be stuck where you are?

Change isn't easy. It's risky. It's uncertain. Our brains are hardwired to resist change because it's unpredictable. We would rather be slightly uncomfortable in a familiar situation than take any chances of being *really* uncomfortable in a situation we've never experienced before.

However, living this way is ultimately frustrating and unfulfilling. Who wants to live with an awareness that it's possible to have a better life without any intention of ever getting there? It's like sitting up in the nosebleed seats when there's an available seat on the 50-yard line that you could have if you wanted. Instead of rushing downstairs to take the better seat, you say, "No thanks. I'd rather stay here where I can't see the players without binoculars."

Even though change is hard, it's worth the effort, and you'll quickly find that getting started is not as difficult as you think. That's what the Winter Warlock quickly learned. After he says he isn't sure he can change, Kris Kringle laughs and says, "Why look here, changing from bad to good is as easy as taking the first step."

If you've seen the movie before, the music is already starting to play in your head. After he tells the Warlock how easy it is to change, Kris begins singing this song:

"Put one foot in front of the other, and soon you'll be walking across the floor.

Put one foot in front of the other, and soon you'll be walking out the door.

You'll never get where you're going if you never get up on your feet.

Come on, there's a good tailwind blowing! A fast-walking man is hard to beat."

Something cool happens inside the Warlock as he's listening to Kris sing this song. He looks at his reflection in a wall of ice and says, "If I want to change the reflection I see in the mirror each morning, you mean that it's just my election to vote for a chance to be reborn?" [16] What's true for the Warlock is true for each of us. Your future is a blank canvas, and you hold the paintbrush.

If you visit our Chick-fil-A's Grow University website at www.growuniversitychickfila.com, I imagine the first thing you'll see is this quote: "The journey of 1,000 miles begins with one step." This message is near and dear to my heart. The road ahead is long and unpredictable, but it starts by simply putting one foot in front of the other. If you're willing to do this, you don't have to stay where you are.

Taking the first step may seem like a small decision at the moment, but it has the potential to make an extraordinary difference. In the 2011 movie "We Bought a

---

[16] The wording here is definitely confusing, but remember, this was the 1970s. People were still wearing bell-bottoms and going to the disco on Friday night. If you're a millennial or Gen-Zer and don't know what I'm talking about, ChatGPT can help you out.

Zoo" starring Matt Damon and Scarlett Johansson, Benjamin Mee (Damon's character) says, "Sometimes all you need is 20 seconds of insane courage, just literally 20 seconds of embarrassing bravery, and I promise you something great will come of it."

There's a moment when Peter chooses to step out of the boat and walks to Jesus on the water. There's a moment when James and John drop their nets and take the first step toward their new rabbi, Jesus. There's a moment when Paul gets up on the road to Damascus, unable to see where he's going but knowing something greater awaits him when he arrives because someone greater is calling him forward. Each man wasn't entirely sure what would happen next, but they still made the decision to put one foot in front of the other.

Your first step matters. Just ask Neil Armstrong about what a difference one small step can make. And over time, one step will turn into ten, one hundred, and ten thousand. Before you know it, you'll look back and be amazed at how far you've traveled, but you'll never get there unless you take the first step.

That said, you might need some extra encouragement to keep going along the way. This doesn't diminish your attitude or abilities in any way. Remember what you read in Chapter Ten – we all need each other. In addition to surrounding yourself with people who will encourage you, challenge you, and make you better, I also invite you to join me on "The Pursuit" blog[17] at our Grow U. website, where I'll write weekly posts designed to help you

---

[17] https://growuniversitychickfila.com/blog

continue taking steps toward the life God has called you to live.

I'll leave you with the same blessing that Paul offers the church in Philippi in Philippians 1:4-6 (NLT): "Whenever I pray, I make my requests for all of you with joy, for you have been my partners in spreading the Good News about Christ from the time you first heard it until now. And I am certain that God, who began the good work within you, will continue his work until it is finally finished on the day when Christ Jesus returns."

Let's go forward on our Never-Ending Pursuit together, and I hope to see you somewhere on the road ahead.

WORKBOOK FOR SMALL GROUP DISCUSSION

A friend once told me, "If you want to run fast, run alone. If you want to run far, run with a friend." I love this quote. As we talked about extensively in Chapter Ten, we're made to live life in community, and we'll be much better off if we invest in others who are challenging us and encouraging us to become our best selves in Christ.

This book will have the greatest impact if you work through each chapter with others. You can read it with your spouse, a few close friends, a team at work, a Bible class, or a small group at church. To help facilitate your conversations, I've created discussion guides that correspond with each chapter. These prompts go beyond the application questions you read at the end of each chapter and help you consider how you can better understand and apply the concepts you're reading about throughout the book.

Remember to cover each meeting in prayer as you invite God to do something incredible in your life and in the lives of others. When we have team meetings at work, I begin each meeting by reading Proverbs 16:3 (NLT): "Commit your actions to the Lord, and your plans will succeed." I see this principle as being critical to our success, and I love how it gives us an opportunity to live out Proverbs 3:5-6, NLT "Trust in the Lord with all your heart; do not depend on your own understanding. Seek his will in all you do, and he will show you which path to take." and Matthew 6:33, NLT "Seek the Kingdom of God above all else, and live righteously, and he will give you everything you need." Keep these verses in mind as you work through this material, and you won't lose sight of your purpose and what you're trying to accomplish together (with God's help, of course).

Feel free to adapt these discussion guides based on your group's unique age, context, and preferences. My hope is that the words you read in this book lead to rich discussions where each person is able to better identify and embrace God's calling on their life.

Introduction: The Secret to True Happiness

Open in prayer:

- Ask God to bless your group's time together, both in today's discussion and throughout all of your meetings. Consider reading Proverbs 3:5-6 and Matthew 6:33 beforehand to fully prepare your heart and mind for what lies ahead.
- Pray that each person would have an open mind and an open heart toward the new direction where God might be leading.

Begin by talking about how your group will interact with each other:

- How often will our group meet?
- Will we meet at the same time and place each week?
- What's expected of each person before, during, and after the discussion?
- How can we support each other throughout this entire journey? (Prayer, accountability, encouragement, gentle challenge, etc.)
- This past week, we read the introduction to the book. What was the main takeaway for you? What was most encouraging and/or challenging?

Continue discussing the book's introduction:

- Think about a time when you experienced happiness after a certain accomplishment or achievement. How long did that feeling last?

- Why do you think people confuse happiness with reaching a destination? How did David challenge this misconception in the first chapter?
- What does David mean when he says, "There is no happiness without the pursuit?" How can embracing this Never-Ending Pursuit lead to a more fulfilling life?
- When you think about life as a journey rather than a destination, how does that shift your perspective on personal growth and fulfillment?
- What role does our faith in God play in our lifelong pursuit of personal growth and development?

Read Psalm 16:11 (NLT) as a group: "You will show me the way of life, granting me the joy of your presence and the pleasures of living with you forever."

The Never-Ending Pursuit Challenge Questions:

- As you think about shifting your perspective on happiness from a destination to a journey, how do you think this might impact your daily life?
- What's one area of life where you've been waiting for a specific outcome? How can you find greater joy in the process?
- Think about a recent challenge you faced. How did you grow through that experience? What lessons did you learn?
- How can you prepare your heart and mind so that you reap the greatest benefit from this book and these discussions?

Close in prayer. Ask God to help each person find joy in The Never-Ending Pursuit. Pray that each person would be transformed more into the image of Christ as they discover how to apply the Biblical principles in this book.

Chapter One: Determine Your Purpose

Open in prayer. Ask God to help each person avoid distractions and focus on the discussion. Consider reading Proverbs 16:3 (NLT) and dedicate your discussion time to the Lord in prayer.

This past week, we read Chapter One of the book. What was the main takeaway for you? What was most encouraging and/or challenging?

Continue discussing the chapter:

- David mentions switching majors multiple times in college and struggling to find his career path. Have you ever experienced a time of major uncertainty in your own life?
- What events throughout your life have helped you discover your purpose?
- Think back on Paul's journey to Damascus when he met Jesus for the first time. How does this story inspire you to continue seeking your own purpose?
- David quotes Frederick Buechner in the chapter, who says that purpose often lies at the intersection between your passion and the world's greatest need. What clues could this provide about your purpose?
- Have you ever felt fear or uncertainty as you considered what your purpose might be? How did you (or could you) overcome that fear?
- How does an awareness of God's presence impact your willingness to embrace your purpose and

pursue your calling despite fear, challenges, and obstacles?

Read Ephesians 2:10 (NLT) as a group: "For we are God's masterpiece. He has created us anew in Christ Jesus, so we can do the good things he planned for us long ago."

The Never-Ending Pursuit Challenge Questions:

- How will you continue to work to discover your unique, God-given purpose over the next several days and weeks?
- If you already know what your purpose is, how well are you living out this purpose? What else could you do to connect your purpose to your thoughts, actions, and decisions?

Close in prayer. Thank God for blessing each person with a unique purpose, and ask for the Holy Spirit's help in discovering and applying each person's purpose.

Chapter Two: Defining Your Core Values

Open in prayer. Thank God for the growth each person has already experienced through the group discussions, and pray that He will continue to bless your time together.

This past week, we read Chapter Two of the book. What was the main takeaway for you? What was most encouraging and/or challenging?

Discussion questions

- Take a moment to reflect on Jesus' core values mentioned in the chapter (integrity, forgiveness, humility, inclusion, service, and sacrifice). Which of these values resonates with you the most? Can you share a personal experience that reflects that value?
- David talks about Chick-fil-A's core values in the chapter. Have you ever thought about the idea that a company's purpose could go beyond making money? How could that impact the people who work for that organization?
- How clear are you about your own personal core values? Do you have a sense of what your values might be?
- How does the story of Joseph inspire you to uphold your own core values even in the face of adversity? Can you think of any modern-day stories of individuals who experienced something difficult without compromising their values?

Read Matthew 4:1-11 as a group. Discuss how Jesus held true to His values despite facing temptation in the wilderness.

The Never-Ending Pursuit Challenge Questions:

- How would your life be different if your core values played a role in every decision you made?
- What's something you could do over the course of the next week to better embody or reflect your values?
- How could you help someone else clarify and live out their values?

Close in prayer. Ask God to align your values with His values and to make your values clear to you so you can begin practicing them more often.

Chapter Three: Setting Meaningful Goals

Open in prayer. Thank God for his constant love, blessing, and provision. Ask God to draw near to your group this week.

This past week, we read Chapter Three of the book. What was the main takeaway for you? What was most encouraging and/or challenging?

Discussion questions

- Picture yourself in ten years. What does your life look like? What do you want to be different? Think about each domain on the "Wheel of Life" (spiritual, physical, mental, personal, family, financial, and career).
- When you think about the elements in Zig Ziglar's "Wheel of Life," which area of life do you feel is the strongest for you right now? Which one could use some work?
- How can we use our goals to serve and elevate others in the same way that Jesus elevated Zacchaeus?
- Think about a time when you failed to reach a goal. What did you learn from that experience? How did you find value from that shortcoming, even if you didn't meet your original goal?

Read Isaiah 43:18-19 (NLT) as a group: "But forget all that—it is nothing compared to what I am going to do. For I am about to do something new. See, I have already begun! Do you not see it? I will make a pathway through the wilderness. I will create rivers in the dry wasteland."

The Never-Ending Pursuit Challenge Questions:

- What are 1-3 goals you could set that align with your purpose and values discussed in previous weeks?
- How will pursuing goals strengthen your relationship with God and your other key life domains?
- How will you stay on track toward reaching your goals? What reinforcements or accountability do you need to put in place?

Close in prayer. Ask God to bless each person with strength and determination as they pursue their goals. Pray that you would set goals that honor God and make His name known.

Chapter Four: Finding and Maintaining Motivation

Open in prayer. Thank God for giving you the strength to live each day, and ask that He will continue to provide you with the motivation you need to live for Him.

This past week, we read Chapter Four of the book. What was the main takeaway for you? What was most encouraging and/or challenging?

Discussion questions

- How have you understood motivation in the past? How did this chapter challenge those preconceived notions?
- What role has motivation played in your life in the past? How aware were you of what was taking place?
- What do you see as the relationship between motivation and discipline? How specifically could you maximize your motivation by building greater discipline?
- What internal motivators are most prevalent in your life? How do they impact your decisions and actions?
- How can understanding the role of dopamine in anticipation and reward help you make more intentional decisions about the activities you pursue in your life?

Read Psalm 37:4-5 (NLT) as a group: "Take delight in the Lord, and he will give you your heart's desires. Commit everything you do to the Lord. Trust him, and he will help you." Discuss how this verse relates to motivation.

The Never-Ending Pursuit Challenge Questions:

- How can you leverage your motivation to pursue the goals you talked about last week? What practical difference will that make in your life this week?
- How can you stay focused on your long-term motivation in a way that helps you make the right decisions in the short term?
- What can you do to remain aware of how you are using and applying your motivation?

Close in prayer. Ask God to give you awareness and clarity about your deepest motivations so that you can live with greater purpose and intention.

Chapter Five: Cultivating Character

Open in prayer. Pray that God would reveal the character traits He wants you to embody and ask for His help in putting them into practice.

This past week, we read Chapter Five of the book. What was the main takeaway for you? What was most encouraging and/or challenging?

Discussion questions

- How did the garden analogy for character development resonate with you personally?
- If you took a look at your current character "garden," what plants do you see growing? What weeds do you notice?
- How do you address weeds on an ongoing basis? How could you do this more intentionally or effectively?
- How does your environment help you develop a stronger character? What changes could you make to improve your surroundings?
- In your opinion, what does it mean to have a growth mindset? How would you know if your mindset was a growth mindset or a fixed mindset?

Read Galatians 5:22-23 as a group. Ask each person to identify 1-2 Fruits of the Spirit that they would like to work on developing.

The Never-Ending Pursuit Challenge Questions:

- What practical steps do you need to take in the short-term to enhance your character development?
- What will you do to better embody the 1-2 Fruits of the Spirit you said you planned to work on developing?
- How can you involve others in the process of character growth and development so that you get the best possible results?

Close in prayer. Pray that God will give you the strength and courage you need to shape your character in a way that reflects Him.

Chapter Six: Pursuing Integrity

Open in prayer. Ask that God would enhance your desire for integrity and be with you as you pursue integrity in your everyday life.

This past week, we read Chapter Six of the book. What was the main takeaway for you? What was most encouraging and/or challenging?

Discussion questions

- What does integrity mean to you? What role does integrity play in your Never-Ending Pursuit?
- Can you think of a time in your life when you did the right thing for the wrong reason? What was the outcome?
- How does the story of the Good Samaritan reflect the principle of living with integrity in the modern-day world? If you applied this story to your own life, what would be the impact?
- David redefines success in this chapter, saying it has more to do with the process and less to do with the result. How would your life be different if you adopted this belief?

Read Galatians 6:9-10 as a group. Consider what these verses say about living with integrity and pursuing the greater good.

The Never-Ending Pursuit Challenge Questions:

- How can you practice greater integrity in your everyday life? What impact would this have on yourself and those around you?

- Who could help you live a life of greater integrity? How will you involve this person?
- Is there anything you feel convicted of in your life because you didn't act with integrity? What can you do to make it right?

Close in prayer. Ask for God to help you and guide you as you seek to live a life of greater integrity.

Chapter Seven: Developing Leadership Skills

Open in prayer. Ask God to inform and deepen your perspective on leadership so that you can become the leader He's called you to be.

This past week, we read Chapter Seven of the book. What was the main takeaway for you? What was most encouraging and/or challenging?

Discussion questions

- What does the idea of "leading yourself" mean to you? What does this concept look like in your life?
- How does leading yourself impact your ability to lead others?
- What makes trust and respect important within leadership? You can't force people to trust and respect you, but how can you become a person worthy of greater trust and respect?
- How does courage play a role in leadership, and how does your faith impact the amount of courage you have?

Read Mark 10:42-45 and Matthew 20:25-28. How do these passages shape our understanding of Jesus as a leader? What do we learn about leadership from Jesus' example?

The Never-Ending Pursuit Challenge Questions:

- What steps will you take this week to lead based on Jesus' example? What impact do you think this will produce?
- In what situations or circles do you need to step up as a leader?

- How will you care for yourself so that you're in the best possible position to lead?

Close in prayer. Ask God to reveal the situations where strong Christian leadership is needed, and pray that He'll give you the courage to step up and lead.

Chapter Eight: Leading with a Servant Heart

Open in prayer. Thank God for Jesus' tremendous example of servant leadership and ask that He would help you follow in Jesus' footsteps.

This past week, we read Chapter Eight of the book. What was the main takeaway for you? What was most encouraging and/or challenging?

Discussion questions

- Think about a leader from your past who you admire. What did you appreciate about this person?
- Have you ever thought about leadership as service? How does this change the way you see leadership?
- If Christian leadership requires self-sacrifice, how does this change your understanding of what it means to lead? What does this look like, practically speaking?
- How does the idea of "changing your mind" connect with the call to lead yourself and lead others? What will this step require of you?
- What do we learn about leadership from the story of David and Mephibosheth? How can you lead in a similar way?

Read Matthew 20:20-28 as a group. What does this story say about Jesus' perspective on glory and honor? How does it shape the way that we think about leading like Jesus led?

The Never-Ending Pursuit Challenge Questions:

- How will you lead with a servant's heart this week? Get as specific as possible.
- What people, situations, and issues could most benefit from servant leadership? Are you the right person to impact these situations? If not, who could have a positive presence?
- How will you continue to remind yourself of this unique understanding of leadership so that you can embody this concept on a consistent basis?

Close in prayer. Ask God to give you the humility you need to serve and lead like Jesus.

Chapter Nine: Navigating Challenges and Obstacles

Open in prayer. Ask that God will help you reshape your understanding of challenges and obstacles so that you can extract as much value as possible from adversity.

This past week, we read Chapter Nine of the book. What was the main takeaway for you? What was most encouraging and/or challenging?

Discussion questions

- How do you typically feel when you experience challenges? How do you respond?
- Think about a challenge you faced recently. What was that process like? How did you overcome it, and what impact did it have on you?
- What's one challenge in your life that contributed to your development in a significant way? How did it have an impact?
- What's an important "stone of remembrance" in your life? What event does that stone help you remember?

Read James 1:2-4 as a group. How can you adopt this attitude when facing trials? What difference would this make?

The Never-Ending Pursuit Challenge Questions:

- How can you reframe challenges as they arise so that they don't derail your Never-Ending Pursuit?
- Just like the Israelites erected physical stones of remembrance, how can you construct a memorial to remind you of what God has done in your life?
- What difference can your "stones of remembrance" make as you look back on your past and think about what you've experienced? Get specific here. When you look back on these events, how can they continue to make a difference?

Close in prayer. Ask God to give each person in the group the strength to face challenges head-on and the ability to appreciate the work God is doing in their lives when they face adversity.

Chapter Ten: Building Positive Relationships

Open in prayer. Thank God for the relationships in your life, and ask that each relationship would be one that honors Him.

This past week, we read Chapter Ten of the book. What was the main takeaway for you? What was most encouraging and/or challenging?

Discussion questions

- What do you think about God looking at creation before relationships and saying that this was "not good?" How does this proclamation impact our lives today?
- Do you find yourself gravitating more toward individualism or communal living? How helpful - or harmful - is this tendency?
- Think about the three main benefits David mentions in the context of relationships. Which one makes the greatest difference in your life? Which one do you feel is currently lacking?
- How does God's love influence the way that you love others? How effectively are you loving others as God has loved you?

Read 1 Corinthians 13 as a group. How can we better adopt this perspective on love and let it inform the way that we love others?

The Never-Ending Pursuit Challenge Questions:

- What are 1-2 relationships in your life that you would like to further invest in? How will you do this? When will you start?
- How can you set healthy boundaries to safeguard your values and avoid distraction or temptation?
- How will you surround yourself with people who help you become the best version of yourself? What practical steps do you need to take?

Close in prayer. Ask for God's help in loving others, even when it's not easy.

Chapter Eleven: Sustaining Growth and Transformation

Open in prayer. Ask that God will give you the stamina needed to sustain the work you've been discussing and practicing over the last several weeks.

This past week, we read Chapter Eleven of the book. What was the main takeaway for you? What was most encouraging and/or challenging?

Discussion questions

- How does the story of the Tortoise and the Hare impact your approach to personal growth?
- What did you think about the disciples' perception of who Jesus was? How did this impact the way they experienced Jesus' death and resurrection?
- How do you interpret Jesus' teachings on suffering and glory? What would it look like for you to apply this perspective in your own life?
- What were your thoughts on The Abide Factor? How could this framework play a meaningful role in your daily life?
- What would it look like for you to pursue excellence as the highest standard? How would that change the way you're currently living?

Read Matthew 25:31-46. What does this passage teach about sustained growth and transformation? How can we apply this passage?

The Never-Ending Pursuit Challenge Questions:

- What habits could help you continue making progress in your relationship with God and your Never-Ending Pursuit? When will you start these habits, and how will you stay on track?
- How can you shift your mindset so that you're able to consistently take up your cross and follow Jesus?
- What opportunities is God giving you right now for growth and transformation? How will you act on these?

Close in prayer. Ask for God to be with you throughout the entire journey, constantly equipping you to take meaningful steps forward.

Conclusion: Making it Stick

Open in prayer. Thank God for the progress you've made as a group over the last several weeks. Ask for God's help in finishing well.

This past week, we read the conclusion of the book. What was the main takeaway for you? What was most encouraging and/or challenging?

Discussion questions

- Why do you think people are so resistant to change?
- Think about a time when you embraced change and uncertainty. What was the impact? How did that experience benefit you?
- How did the illustration from "Santa Claus is Comin' to Town" resonate with you? Where do you think one step could have a noticeable impact?
- As David says on his Grow University website, "The journey of 1,000 miles begins with one step." Now that you have a first step in mind, where do you think God might lead you 1,000 steps from now? Try to dream big here!

Read Philippians 1:3-6 as a group. How can this passage inspire and motivate you to continue pursuing change?

The Never-Ending Pursuit Challenge Questions:

- How do you feel like you've grown since reading this book? What's been the biggest change in you?
- What's next for you? Where do you still need to stretch or improve?
- What have you learned from reading the book and from your group's time together? What do you want to hang onto?

Close in prayer. Thank God for the time your group has had together, and ask for his continued blessing and involvement as you move forward in your Never-Ending Pursuit.

All Bible verses taken from the New Living Translation (NLT) unless otherwise stated.

REFERENCES

Introduction: The Secret to True Happiness

Hebrews 12:1

2 Peter 1:5-8

Chapter One: Determine Your Purpose

Acts 9:15-16

Philippians 3:5-6

Wishful Thinking: A Seeker's ABC by Frederick Buechner, HarperOne; Expanded edition (1993)

2 Timothy 1:7 NKJV

Judges 6:13

Chapter Two: Defining Your Core Values

Chick-fil-A company core values page (https://www.chick-fil-a.com/about/who-we-are)

The Pursuit blog (https://growuniversitychickfila.com/blog/)

The Advantage by Patrick Lencioni, Jossey-Bass; 1st edition (2012)

Chapter Three: Setting Meaningful Goals

Zig Ziglar's "Wheel of Life" - https://www.ziglar.com/articles/the-wheel-of-life/

Luke 19:10

Atomic Habits by James Clear, Avery; First Edition (2018)

Chapter Four: Finding and Maintaining Motivation

The Power of Positive Thinking by Norman Vincent Peale, EBURY PRESS (2004)

The Seven Habits of Highly Effective People by Stephen Covey, Simon & Schuster; Anniversary edition (2020)

EntreLeadership by Dave Ramsey, Howard Books; Illustrated edition (2011)

The Craig Groeschel Leadership Podcast - https://podcasts.apple.com/us/podcast/craig-groeschel-leadership-podcast/id1070649025

Chapter Five: Cultivating Character

Matthew 13:3-9, 18-23

Do Over by Jon Acuff, Portfolio; Reprint edition (2017)

Life Is 10% What Happens to You and 90% How You React by Chuck Swindoll, Thomas Nelson (2023)

Proverbs 9:8

Galatians 5:22-23

Matthew 13:24-30

James 5:7-8

Chapter Six: Pursuing Integrity

Luke 10:21, 30-37

Galatians 6:9-10

Chapter Seven: Developing Leadership Skills

Luke 16:10

Proverbs 11:25

Chapter Eight: Leading with a Servant Heart

Matthew 20:26-28

Switch on Your Brain by Dr. Caroline Leaf, Baker Books; 8.2.2013 edition (2013)

Romans 12:1

Philippians 4:8

2 Samuel 9:7

"Carried to the Table" by Leeland, *Sound of Melodies*, 2006

Chapter Nine: Navigating Challenges and Obstacles

2 Corinthians 5:21

Romans 8:28

Romans 5:3-5

James 1:2-4

"Grace is Greater" by Kyle Idelman

Evan Almighty, 2007

1 Samuel 7:12

The Money Pit, 1986

"Bad Blood," Taylor Swift

The Count of Monte Cristo, 2002

Chapter Ten: Building Positive Relationships

"Ted Lasso," 2020

Genesis 2:18

Proverbs 27:17

John 13:34

1 John 4:19

Boy Meets World, Disney Channel, American Broadcasting Company (1993-2000)

The Power of the Other by Dr. Henry Cloud, HarperBusiness (1885)

Ecclesiastes 4:12

Necessary Endings by Dr. Henry Cloud, Harper Business; 12/19/10 edition (2011)

1 Corinthians 15:33

2 Timothy 4:7-8

Chapter Eleven: Sustaining Growth and Transformation

Mark 8:27-28, 30-34

Galatians 6:9

John 16:33

The Abide Factor by Shawn Lyons, David Grimm, and Nate Long, 40 Day Publishing (2023)

Conclusion: Making it Stick

Santa Claus is Comin' to Town, 1970

We Bought a Zoo, 2011

Philippians 1:4-6

All Bible verses are taken from the New Living Translation (NLT) unless otherwise stated.

ABOUT THE AUTHOR

David Grimm and his wife, Kelly, own Chick-fil-A on University Avenue in West Des Moines, Iowa. David and Kelly have been in the restaurant business since 2011. They opened Chick-fil-A in 2015 and have grown the University Avenue location by more than 350% since they started. David is incredibly thankful for his top-notch team, and the remarkable guest experience they provide on a daily basis. Since 2015, his location has donated roughly $1 million to the community and team through food donations, support, and education assistance.

In addition to this book, David is the co-author of *The Abide Factor: A Biblically-based approach to living an abundant life and bearing fruit in Christ,* and he looks forward to the release of his autobiography, *Unlikely Candidate,* in the near future.

David and Kelly love being able to live out their faith through their words and deeds every day. They have four children and live in West Des Moines, Iowa.

For more information go to AuthorDavidGrimm.com.